OUR AMERICAN DREAM
COOKBOOK

OUR
AMERICAN DREAM
COOKBOOK

**FAVORITE RECIPES & THE INSPIRING JOURNEYS
OF 80 CULINARY TRAILBLAZERS FROM
SAMUEL ADAMS BREWING THE AMERICAN DREAM**

By
JENNIFER GLANVILLE LOVE

Foreword
JIM KOCH
SAMUEL ADAMS FOUNDER & BREWER

Photography
MICHAEL PIAZZA

Salty Days Media Company LLC
98 Forest Avenue
Cohasset, MA 02025

First published in the United States by Salty Days Media Company LLC 2024

Library of Congress Cataloging-in-Publication Data
Name: Glanville Love, Jennifer
Title: *Our American Dream Cookbook: Favorite Recipes & The Inspiring Journeys of 80 Culinary Trailblazers from Samuel Adams Brewing The American Dream*/Jennifer Glanville Love
Identifiers: LCCN 2024937980 (print)/ISBN 9798990485600 (hardcover)

ISBN: 979-8-9904856-0-0

Publisher **Sara Domville**

Editorial Director **Kim Laidlaw**

Creative Director **Alexandra Zeigler**

Assistant Designer **Diana Heom**

Photographer **Michael Piazza**

Photo Assistants **Andreana Kraft & Dan Orlow**

Food Stylist **Christine Tobin**

Food Stylist Assistants **Rachel Michel & Laura Sui**

Writer & Brand Advisor **Marta Loeb**

Writer **Shirley Fairclough**

Production Manager **Chris Hemesath**

Distributed by Simon & Schuster Publishing Services
1 (800) 223-2336

Printed in China

You too can realize your own dream of food and beverage entrepreneurship. Learn more about Brewing the American Dream at www.brewingtheamericandream.com.

Cover Photograph: Beef Chili with Beans (page 85)

Why We Love Salty Days . . .

In ancient Rome, salt was so precious that it served as currency, giving rise to the term "salary." Essential for flavoring and preserving food, salt ensured sustenance year-round, preventing waste and enhancing taste.

Today, we celebrate a modern twist on the concept of salty days. These are the moments in life that we cherish and savor. Salty days are filled with delicious tastes, delightful scents, fabulous feelings, and exquisite sounds. Amidst life's challenges, these memorable moments often involve our favorite people engaging in beloved activities or embarking on exciting new adventures such as the launch of this new publishing company, Salty Days Media Company.

Founder and Publisher Sara Domville spearheaded this innovative publishing venture—dedicated to partnering with esteemed brands and entrepreneurs—to produce books, content, TV, video, and ecommerce opportunities that inspire, entertain, and bring joy to all. For more information, reach out to Sara at saradomville@saltydays.com.

CONTENTS

"I want to enable people to do something that conventional wisdom suggests they would not be able to do."

—Jim Koch, Samuel Adams Founder & Brewer

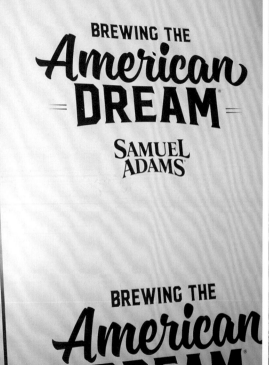

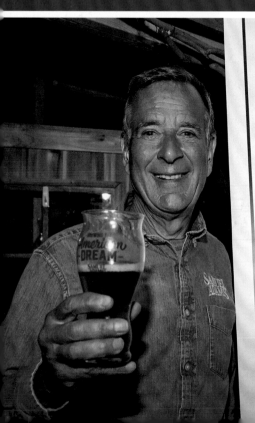

BREWING THE
American
DREAM

SAMUEL
ADAMS

BREWING THE
American
DREAM

FOREWORD

Ask any business owner—starting a business has an element of terror. It's like a trapeze artist working without a net. Whether it's a tech start-up or a mom-and-pop shop, it takes guts.

As I embarked on my own entrepreneurial journey, I debated what was scary versus dangerous. To me, leaving a cushy job in consulting to start a brewery was scary, but it wasn't dangerous. I wanted to build something, and beer was in my blood. I'm a sixth-generation brewer after all. What was dangerous to me then, and posed a real risk to my livelihood, was staying in a job that didn't inspire or fulfill me.

So in 1984, now some forty years ago, I started a beer company. With my great-great-grandfather's German beer recipe in hand, I set out to challenge the status quo with the highest-quality and freshest beer on the market. One of the dependable rules in business is this: if you're going to bring out a new product, it must be better or cheaper than what's on the market.

I had an MBA, so in theory, I knew how to run a business. But I didn't know squat. I didn't know the basics, like how to set up a payroll or keep track of sales or inventory. That's where the terror seeped back in. I made mistakes and I got some good advice, but, looking back, it was trial and error.

Cut to 2008. Boston Beer Company was doing well and growing beyond our flagship Samuel Adams. We wanted to give back in a way that went beyond making rogue donations or rolling up our sleeves for charity work. I wanted to honor our roots, our coworkers, and our community. Enter Samuel Adams Brewing the American Dream. I thought about what food and beverage entrepreneurs like me really needed to take the scary jump into pursuing their passions. Sure, it was access to capital, but more than that, it was nuts-and-bolts business advice.

We started small in Boston, pairing food and beverage entrepreneurs with Boston Beer Company coworkers as mentors and valuable sounding boards. We began underwriting a loan program to provide equitable access to modest business loans. We made a big impact in our local small business community, and it felt great. Entrepreneurs wear many hats, and we offered the expertise of our roughly one thousand coworkers to navigate everything from packaging to selling to averting disasters. We gave fledgling companies a leg to stand on and a leg up in business.

Since then, Brewing the American Dream has expanded nationally and increased support to entrepreneurs in food, beverage, hospitality, and brewing. We have counseled more than fifteen thousand current and prospective entrepreneurs and funded more than $100 million in loans while providing over $500,000 in grants through programs like the Pitch Room. I love our Brewing & Business Experienceship in particular for its unconventional nature: a brewer with 1 percent of market share (Samuel Adams) hosts a national competition to provide unparalleled support, unlimited coaching, and unbelievable collaboration to a craft brewery competing for a piece of that very same pie.

Over the last fifteen years, we have worked with thousands of entrepreneurs whose stories are as inspiring as their offerings are delicious. We wanted to create a cookbook in celebration of how far we've come together and to inspire even more makers to go with the scary choice and follow their dream. While the recipes here run the gamut, a few ingredients are consistent throughout: passion, commitment, and diligence.

Jim Koch

—Jim Koch, Samuel Adams Founder & Brewer

"America is built on the dreams and triumphs of people who took a chance to pursue something better. Since 2008, we have helped hardworking, passionate food and beverage craftspeople succeed so they can do what they love: provide for their families, create local jobs, and help grow vibrant communities. Because, as we see it, we're all in this together. For Samuel Adams, it's not just about brewing a better beer, it's about waking up every day to do something you love."

—Jennifer Glanville Love, Samuel Adams Brewer and Director of Partnerships at The Boston Beer Company, overseeing Brewing the American Dream

HOW IT ALL BEGAN

Many small businesses begin in the founder's kitchen or garage or on the dining-room table, and Samuel Adams was no exception. Jim Koch brewed his first batch of Samuel Adams Boston Lager on his kitchen stove at his home in Newton, Massachusetts, as the initial step in realizing his dream of starting a brewery while still working as a business consultant. Home brewing wasn't novel, but it was new to Jim, and even with a family recipe and textbook research, he encountered side effects. The steam from the boil caused the kitchen wallpaper to peel off the walls, and some of the beer bottles aging in his cellar soon exploded. He wrote most of his initial business plan not at a dining-room table but at thirty thousand feet while traveling for his day job.

Several successful brews later, Jim bootstrapped Boston Beer Company in 1984 and took a true homegrown approach to launching the Samuel Adams brand. Inspired by his time at the outdoor education program Outward Bound, which stresses both exploring personal potential and collaboration with others, Jim dubbed his approach to frugality his String Theory, which maintains that creativity and teamwork will outperform big budgets. He devoted virtually all his seed capital to making the best beer possible, from quality ingredients to renting time in a world-class brewery. The rest would follow.

In the company's early days, he didn't allocate money for marketing (or even office space), relying instead on the one resource he had, his beer. Jim saw every bottle of Samuel Adams as a billboard and set out to get it in as many hands as possible. From personally approaching customers to creating the first table-tent advertisements at bars, Jim was committed to making Samuel Adams Boston Lager a household name, even though it was a beer few people had heard of at the time.

Visibility of this fledgling company took a great leap forward on June 1, 1985, just six weeks after Jim made his first Boston Lager deliveries to local bars and restaurants along the city's famous Freedom Trail. He and his founding partner, Rhonda Kallman, had flown to Denver to attend an event called the Great American Beer Festival, where industry titans and beer lovers converged to sample and score a myriad of beers. Big breweries had fancy booths. Small Colorado microbreweries had loyal customers. But when all the votes were counted, Samuel Adams had won first place.

Soon after taking the top award at the festival, Samuel Adams took off, and Boston Beer Company was flying high. Bar managers who were previously "too busy" for Jim were now ordering cases and putting neon Samuel Adams beacons in their windows. The term "microbrew" gave way to "craft beer," with breweries like Samuel Adams pushing the limits of what defines micro. The new category spoke to the real craft that goes into brewing and the industry's built-in community. Jim is regularly credited with starting the craft-beer revolution because of his focus on quality and of standing up to the big guys. In the forty years of Samuel Adams, the number of craft breweries in the United States has grown from under fifty to over ninety-five hundred.

Despite the comparatively meteoric growth of craft, it still accounted for less than 1 percent of the American beer business, which was ultimately ruled by big imports. Jim would say, "They spill more beer than we make," and he was right. But craft brewers were gaining momentum, and despite challenges from larger breweries, craft continued to grow for the better part of the decade.

Craft beer eventually hit a brick wall in the 1990s however, and the smaller players leveled out with countless mergers, acquisitions, and disappearances dotting the craft-beer map. The next challenge for Jim was adjusting to a new world order and committing to the long haul. Samuel Adams was growing nationally, and in 1997, Jim and his team bought the historic Hudepohl-Schoenling brewery in Cincinnati, where his father had once worked as an apprentice, to further Boston Beer Company's commitment to delivering the freshest beer possible. Jim invested in his coworkers and developed a best-in-class sales force that continues to be recognized as a top performer in the industry.

In his book *Quench Your Own Thirst*, Jim talks about "growing when you're not growing." When craft beer took off again in 2004, the company was shored up, poised for growth, and ready to roll! When business slows, smart leaders ask, "What can we improve now while we have the 'bandwidth'?"

At a time when rapid growth was demanding all of Boston Beer Company's attention, Jim and his coworkers were starting to wonder what was next. When it came to craft beer, "variety" was what was next. In 2008, Samuel Adams created a number of seasonal beers and a series called the Brewmasters Collection. While the big guys were making lighter and lighter beers, Jim's curiosity led him to the darker end of the beer spectrum. He made a Cream Stout, a Double Bock, and then a Triple Bock. That seasonal program set the precedent for rotating

beer styles, and the range of styles cemented Boston Beer Company's craft credentials.

While continuously challenging drinkers' expectations of beer, Jim had quietly started another craft beer movement, this time around extreme beer. Double Bock and Triple Bock were just the start, and then came Millennium and Utopias. These small-batch, big beers redefined what beer could be. Utopias pushed the envelope. Weighing in at 28% ABV, Utopias is a ruby-black, slightly viscous, noncarbonated liquid that is shelf-stable, which means it evolves—and improves—with age. It's best compared to a vintage port or Cognac. In a word, its introduction redefined what a beer could be.

Samuel Adams Utopias has come to occupy a cherished place in the hearts and minds of Boston Beer Company coworkers. It's boundary pushing, mind-blowing, and unlike any other beer. But that's not all. When it's released every two years, the bottles are numbered and then given to every coworker in order of tenure at the company. Jim gets bottle number one, and newer hires get bottles that push four digits. Every person's Utopias number is a point of pride. The latest Utopias releases have been brewed, barreled, aged, and bottled across the Boston Beer Company network, ensuring that coworkers at every brewing location have played a role in this beloved beer.

THE ORIGINAL: SAMUEL ADAMS BOSTON LAGER

First brewed in founder Jim Koch's kitchen in 1984, a time when there were fewer than one hundred breweries in the United States, Samuel Adams Boston Lager helped pave the way for the American craft-beer revolution. From the beginning, the world's finest hand-selected ingredients were used to create this perfectly balanced and complex beer—and that will never change. To this day, Jim

tastes each batch of this signature lager to ensure it meets the high quality standards of the brand. When drinkers pick up a Samuel Adams Boston Lager, they know they're going to experience a rich, delicious full-flavored beer—a beer that is approachable, layered, and smooth, with a harmonious mix of caramel and toffee malt sweetness and distinct noble hops character and aroma.

GIVING BACK & BEYOND

Nurturing and sustaining Boston Beer Company's culture and spirit of cooperation have always been a priority. While the company had hit its stride by 2008, Jim was determined to give back. He participated in an office-wide social-impact outing where coworkers painted a community center in South Boston. The fact that the company spent $10,000 of good management time to do $2,000 of mediocre painting didn't sit well with him. He also knew that simply writing a check to a worthy cause wouldn't add value to the team, customers, or shareholders. Jim sought to bring meaningful contributions to the community. He decided to "stop painting and start partnering."

Enter Samuel Adams Brewing the American Dream, the answer to Jim's quest to transfer the same spirit of entrepreneurship, innovation, and creativity that defines Boston Beer Company's economic mission to its social mission. Launched in 2008, it was designed to provide food, beverage, and hospitality entrepreneurs with the essential ingredients to start, strengthen, and grow their small businesses—something Jim certainly would have benefited from in 1984. Brewing the American Dream was one way to share his knowledge and experience while empowering other entrepreneurs and giving them the tools to overcome whatever challenges lie ahead.

From providing access to capital through Accion Opportunity Fund, Boston Beer Company's longtime lending partner, to offering business-fundamentals coaching through Boston Beer Company coworkers, Brewing the American Dream entrepreneurs were set up for success. This program not only fueled small businesses, but also empowered coworkers and grounded the Samuel Adams brand in a meaningful social-impact cause. It was anything but charity. It was inspiring economic development. And now, more than a decade and a half after its launch, it continues to deliver help to a steadily growing number of small businesses across the country.

Boston Beer Company has also been a model for entrepreneurs to stay ahead of the curve. Beers like Utopias demonstrate the pride Boston Beer Company coworkers feel and reflects the company's commitment to innovation. Creating this unique beer wasn't just about what was next for Samuel Adams. It was also about seeing the forest through the trees and future-proofing the Boston Beer Company business with new entrants in the category. Much as Jim supported new craft brewers through Brewing the American Dream, he fueled and challenged conventions of beer companies by introducing nontraditional alcoholic beverages like hard tea (Twisted Tea), spiked seltzer (Truly Hard Seltzer), and hard cider (Angry Orchard). Boston Beer Company was expanding into new areas to attract new drinkers and also evading cannibalization of its well-established product line.

All these lessons have one common theme, and it's something chefs learn early in their careers. Learn to pivot and adapt. If you run out of rosemary, use thyme. Sour cream gone bad? Substitute yogurt. With a little innovation and creativity, recipes can be adjusted and often improved. It's true for beer, it's true for businesses, and it's true for life. Experiment a little and always take time to smell the hops. *Cheers!*

START-UP
SHAREABLES

Rujak buah is an Indonesian chilled fruit salad of crisp apples, pineapple, watermelon, and mango. You can substitute your favorite fruits for some or all of the ones listed here to create your own version. But what makes this salad extraordinary is the spicy, sour, and sweet sauce that coats the fruit. This recipe comes from **Cyrilla Suwarsa,** cofounder of **Nuts + Nuts** in California, who suggests serving it as an appetizer or side dish, particularly with barbecue and cold beer. Celebrate the vibrant colors, flavors, and textures by assembling the salad in a clear glass bowl.

RUJAK BUAH WITH CHILI LIME CASHEWS

To make the fruit salad, in a serving bowl, combine the apple, pineapple, watermelon, and mango and toss to mix. Cover and refrigerate until well chilled.

To make the cashew topping, when ready to serve, in a small bowl, stir together the palm sugar, salt, and hot water until the sugar and salt dissolve. Transfer the mixture to a mini food processor and add the tamarind paste, red chiles (if using), and cashews. Process until well combined and slightly chunky. Taste and adjust the sugar, salt, and tamarind.

Drizzle the cashew mixture over the chilled fruits, toss to coat evenly, and serve at once.

Note: Prepared tamarind paste can be found at many well-stocked markets. For a more authentic turn, make the tamarind paste by soaking 1½ teaspoons fresh tamarind pulp in 1 tablespoon hot water and then strain the pulp through a fine-mesh sieve.

1 cup peeled and cubed Granny Smith apple, in 1-inch cubes

1 cup cubed fresh pineapple, in 1-inch cubes

1 cup cubed watermelon, in 1-inch cubes

1 cup cubed mango, in 1-inch cubes

6 tablespoons palm sugar or coconut sugar

½ teaspoon fine sea salt

2 tablespoons hot water

1 teaspoon tamarind paste (see Note)

1 or 2 small fresh red chiles or ½ jalapeño chile, minced (optional)

½ cup Nuts + Nuts Chili Lime Cashews or other chile-seasoned cashews

Makes 6 servings

These bite-size appetizers—similar to a sushi roll—start with elegant smoked salmon and quickly take a quirky turn with the addition of crisp, tangy pickle spears and cream cheese. **Sean Chapman** of **Chappy's Pickles** in Charlestown, Massachusetts, invented these inspired pinwheels as a novel way to enjoy familiar flavors in an entirely new form. Perfect for those who love a bit of fun on their plate, these sea-rich roll-ups, which are coated with a toasty mix of sesame and poppy seeds, are a fantastic accompaniment to your favorite beer.

SMOKED SALMON PINWHEELS WITH PICKLES

1 teaspoon sesame seeds

1 teaspoon poppy seeds

4 ounces cold-smoked salmon, thinly sliced

½ cup (about 4 ounces) cream cheese, cut into small pieces, at room temperature

2 tablespoons finely chopped fresh chives

4 dill pickle spears, preferably Chappy's Pickles Dill Garlic Spears

½ ripe but firm avocado, peeled and thinly sliced

1 teaspoon fresh lemon juice

Lay a sheet of parchment paper on a work surface. Sprinkle the sesame seeds and poppy seeds on the parchment, creating a rectangle about 6 by 8 inches, with a longer side facing you. Lay slices of the smoked salmon over the seeds so the seeds stick to the salmon, staying within the 6-by-8-inch rectangle as much as possible.

To layer the filling over the salmon, sprinkle the cream cheese evenly over the salmon. Using a butter knife, gently spread the cream cheese to cover the salmon completely. Sprinkle the chives evenly over the cream cheese. Lay the pickle spears horizontally on the salmon, across the edge of the rectangle that is nearest to you, leaving a ½-inch border from the bottom edge. Then arrange the avocado slices horizontally across the middle of the rectangle. Drizzle the avocado with the lemon juice.

To roll the filled salmon, starting from the edge closest to you with the pickle spears, roll up the salmon into a tight log, using the parchment paper as needed to keep the salmon slices in place. Transfer to the refrigerator to firm up until chilled, about 1 hour.

To cut the log into pinwheels, using a sharp knife, cut the salmon log crosswise into 8 to 10 slices. Arrange the pinwheels cut side up on a plate and serve.

ALWAYS

VEGAN
GLUTEN-FREE
SOY-FREE

LIMITED EDITION
FLAVOR

CAROLYN'S

krisps.

BREWING THE
AMERICAN DREAM
Winner

COOKIE-CRACKERS FOR THE CURIOUS

NET WT 5.3 oz (150g)

CHOCOLATE CHAI

notes: dark chocolate and warming
spices unite, comforting like a hug

AMIE KESLER, FOUNDER OF CAROLYN'S KRISPS

Amie Kesler has long believed that food serves as a universal connector, a tangible expression of care that transcends cultural boundaries and speaks to generations. It has the remarkable ability to initiate conversations, foster relationships, and etch enduring memories. She credits her belief in the transformative potential of food to the influence of the resilient, determined women who shaped her upbringing.

Amie's professional journey has traversed diverse industries, ranging from publishing to start-up insurance technology to retail design and fashion. Despite the obvious variety, a common thread ties these experiences together: the profound significance of fostering connections. In retrospect, it's not surprising that her path has led her to the creation of Carolyn's Krisps, her three-year-old company where food is not just art but also a sensory experience that nurtures community.

Honoring her grandmother Carolyn's cherished snack tradition, Amie revitalized her grandmother's original recipe to create vegan, gluten-free, soy-free Cheddar Krisps. Each bite embodies a harmonious fusion of flavor, texture, and a sprinkle of nostalgia, evoking cherished memories of comfort and joy. This essence of what Amie calls "snack magic" permeates every facet of the business, from hiring to community engagement.

Located in a historically underserved area of Chicago, the manufacturing facility embraces unique hiring practices by providing opportunities for individuals facing barriers to traditional employment. Through this inclusive approach, the company not only crafts delicious snacks but also empowers the employees with invaluable life skills, fostering personal growth and resilience.

"SAMUEL ADAMS REPRESENTS MORE THAN JUST BEER, AND CAROLYN'S KRISPS TRANSCENDS THE REALM OF MERE SNACK. IT EMBODIES A SENSE OF COMMUNITY, EVOKES A FEELING, AND PROVIDES A MEANS TO CONNECT THAT ENRICHES LIVES."

Amie Kesler

The support of the Brewing the American Dream grant has been instrumental in the journey of this young company. It has facilitated the acquisition of equipment, helped expand production capacity, and enabled the establishment of new nationwide retail partnerships.

Walk into any gathering of **Amie Kesler's** family—even for a quick visit—and you're likely to be asked immediately if you are hungry. Before you can answer, snack trays and dips appear. This lemony roasted pepper and white bean dip is an ode to those moments of catching up, hosting, and celebrating. The ingredients are simple, but the flavor is deep, and when paired with her **Carolyn's Krisps** Cheddar Krisps, it's an immediate hit with family and friends.

WHITE BEAN DIP WITH ROASTED RED PEPPERS

4 red bell peppers, halved lengthwise, stemmed, and seeded

1 yellow onion, cut into large chunks

6 garlic cloves, peeled

2 tablespoons olive oil, plus more if needed

1¼ teaspoons fine sea salt

1 teaspoon freshly ground pepper

1 (15½-ounce) can Great Northern beans, drained and rinsed

¼ cup chopped fresh basil leaves

2 tablespoons fresh lemon juice

1 tablespoon nutritional yeast

Carolyn's Cheddar Krisps or your favorite crackers or crudités, for serving

Preheat the oven to 400°F.

To roast the vegetables, pile the bell peppers, onion, and garlic on a sheet pan. Drizzle with the oil, tossing the vegetables to coat them evenly. Season with the salt and pepper. Arrange the peppers, cut side down in a single layer and spread out the garlic cloves and onion pieces. Roast until the bell peppers and onion pieces are blistered, about 30 minutes.

To steam the roasted peppers, transfer them to a bowl and cover with a plate. Set aside to steam just until cool enough to handle, about 10 minutes. Peel the peppers and discard the skins.

To make the dip, transfer the peeled peppers, onion, and garlic to a blender. Add the beans, basil, lemon juice, and nutritional yeast and blend on medium-high speed until smooth, stopping to scrape down the sides of the blender as needed. Drizzle in a bit more oil if needed to achieve a good dip consistency.

Transfer the dip to a serving bowl and serve with the crackers for dipping.

Inspired by his mother's cooking and his Mexican and Los Angeles roots, **Oscar Ochoa** launched **El Machete,** a line of small-batch handcrafted spicy-hot condiments, sauces, and Mexican side dishes, in the early 2010s. Here he shares a smoky, rich salsa of charred tomatillos, creamy avocado, and a pleasantly fiery mix of serrano, jalapeño, and poblano chiles that celebrates the depth and vibrancy of the Mexican kitchen.

CHARRED SALSA VERDE
WITH CHUNKY AVOCADO

1 tablespoon canola oil

1 pound tomatillos, husked and rinsed

1 serrano chile, stemmed

1 jalapeño chile, stemmed

1 poblano chile, stemmed

2 garlic cloves, peeled

1 teaspoon fine sea salt

1 ripe but firm avocado, halved, pitted, peeled, and cubed

1 cup chopped fresh cilantro

Tortilla chips, for serving

To char the vegetables, heat a large frying pan, preferably cast-iron, over high heat until very hot. Add the oil, swirl to coat the bottom of the pan, and then add the tomatillos, chiles, and garlic. Cook, turning about every 3 minutes, until evenly charred and softened, about 5 minutes for the garlic and 8 to 14 minutes for the tomatillos and chiles. Transfer the ingredients to a bowl as they are ready, cover the bowl with a plate, and let steam for 10 minutes.

To puree the salsa, in a blender or food processor, combine the tomatillos, chiles, garlic, and salt and process to your desired texture, adding up to ¼ cup water as needed to loosen the salsa. At this point, the salsa can be transferred to an airtight container and refrigerated for up to 4 days; bring to room temperature before serving.

Just before serving, gently fold in the avocado and cilantro. Serve with chips.

Oven roasting is the secret to this deeply flavorful tomato salsa. It is served with simple yet yummy cheese quesadillas, but it also makes a perfect accompaniment to tacos, tostadas, or Migas with Chorizo (page 115). The recipe comes from chefs **Ken Katz and Jeannette Flores-Katz** of **Buenos Dias Café and Pupuseria** in Atlanta. They suggest you dial the heat in the salsa up or down to your taste and have a cold beer on hand to fully enjoy the experience.

CHEESE QUESADILLAS
WITH ROASTED TOMATO SALSA

To roast the vegetables, preheat the oven to 350°F. Line a sheet pan with aluminum foil.

Arrange the tomatoes cut side down on the prepared sheet pan with the chiles, onion slices, and garlic cloves around them in a single layer. Roast the tomatoes until the skins pull away from the flesh, and the chiles, onion, and garlic are softened, about 15 minutes. Remove from the oven and let cool completely on the pan. Remove and discard the tomato skins.

To puree the salsa, in a blender, combine the roasted tomatoes, chiles, onion, and garlic and blend until smooth. Transfer to a bowl, fold in the avocado, and season with a pinch of salt. Taste and adjust with more salt if needed. Set aside until serving.

To store the salsa, transfer to an airtight container, press a piece of plastic wrap directly onto the surface, top with the cover, and refrigerate for up to 3 days.

To assemble the quesadillas, warm a griddle or large frying pan over medium-low heat. Add the tortillas to the hot surface in a single layer and heat, flipping once, just until pliable, about 30 seconds total. As the tortillas are ready, transfer them to a work surface in a single layer. To fill each quesadilla, spoon 2 tablespoons cheese onto half of each tortilla and fold over the other half to make a half-moon.

To cook the quesadillas, return the griddle or pan to medium-low heat. When it is hot, brush the surface with oil. When the oil is hot, add as many quesadillas as will fit without crowding and cook, turning once, until golden brown on both sides and the cheese is melted, 1 to 1½ minutes on each side. Transfer to a plate and repeat with the remaining quesadillas, brushing the cooking surface with more oil as needed.

Serve the quesadillas hot with the salsa on the side.

Roasted Tomato Salsa

3 large Roma tomatoes, cored and halved lengthwise

1 serrano chile, seeded, deveined, and cut into 3 equal pieces

1 jalapeño chile, seeded, deveined, and cut into 3 equal pieces

½ yellow onion, thickly sliced

4 garlic cloves, peeled

1 large, ripe avocado, halved, pitted, peeled, and diced

Fine sea salt

Quesadillas

12 corn or flour tortillas, about 6 inches in diameter

1½ cups (about 6 ounces) shredded Oaxaca or Monterey jack cheese

Canola or peanut oil, for cooking

Makes about 8 servings

★ BREWER'S FAVORITE ★

We love the slight sweetness that roasted malts and specialty hops add to this creamy beer-and-cheese spread. In the fall, Samuel Adams Brewer and Director of Partnerships **Jennifer Glanville Love** substitutes Samuel Adams OctoberFest, which, with its subtle floral hops and caramel malts, gives the spread a heartier, nuttier flavor. For the best results, start with a block of cheese rather than a preshredded variety and pour the beer into a glass an hour or two prior to assembling the spread so it has time to go flat before you use it. Serve this popular spread with crackers or crusty bread.

BEER CHEESE WITH BOSTON LAGER

To make the cheese spread, in a food processor or blender, combine the cheese, beer, garlic, Worcestershire sauce, hot sauce, salt, and pepper and process until a coarse puree forms. Transfer to a serving dish.

Cover and chill the spread until thickened, for at least 2 hours, before serving. The beer cheese will keep in an airtight container in the refrigerator for up to 2 weeks.

Serve chilled with crackers, pretzels, or bread for scooping.

1½ pounds sharp white Cheddar cheese, shredded

1 (12-ounce) bottle Samuel Adams Boston Lager, flat and at room temperature

2 garlic cloves, minced

2 tablespoons Worcestershire sauce

2 teaspoons hot sauce

¼ teaspoon fine sea salt

¼ teaspoon freshly ground pepper

Crackers, soft pretzels, or sliced crusty bread, for serving

Making your own hummus is quick and rewarding. You'll likely already have the ingredients in your pantry, and your version is sure to be healthier and tastier than its store-bought equivalent. The cumin and ginger in this recipe add extra zing, and a drizzle of olive oil and a sprinkle chopped fresh flat-leaf parsley work well as a finishing touch. Pair this memorable hummus with crunchy Jack's Crackers, which are freshly baked in Keene, New Hampshire, by **Kevin Dremel,** who also gave us this great recipe. At **Jack's Crackers,** a no-fuss philosophy drives production: a cracker is a lot like life. It may be simple, but it doesn't have to be boring.

LEMONY HUMMUS WITH CRACKERS

1 (15-ounce) can chickpeas, drained and rinsed

½ cup tahini

¼ cup fresh lemon juice

2 to 4 tablespoons ice-cold water, plus more if needed

1 tablespoon extra-virgin olive oil, plus more for drizzling

1 garlic clove, roughly chopped

½ teaspoon fine sea salt

½ teaspoon ground cumin

¼ teaspoon ground ginger

Chopped fresh flat-leaf parsley, for garnishing

Jack's Crackers, pita bread, or pita chips, for serving

To make the hummus, in a small food processor or a high-speed blender, combine the chickpeas, tahini, lemon juice, 2 tablespoons of the water, olive oil, garlic, salt, cumin, and ginger. Process on high speed to a smooth puree, stopping the processor once or twice to scrape down the sides. The mixture should be ultrasmooth, pale, and creamy. If the hummus is too thick for your liking, add 1 to 2 tablespoons more ice-cold water to loosen the mixture.

To garnish the hummus, scrape the hummus into a serving bowl or onto a small platter and use a spoon to create nice swooshes on top. Drizzle with olive oil and sprinkle with parsley.

Accompany with the crackers. Leftover hummus will keep in an airtight container in the refrigerator for up to 1 week.

SAMUEL ADAMS
SUMMER ALE

This American wheat ale has a citrusy blend of orange, lemon, and lime peel. We balance this tangy, zesty component with the peppery warmth of grains of paradise, a West African spice related to cardamom and ginger. Crisp, refreshing, and bursting with flavor, our Summer Ale is ideal for ditching the hustle and turning any summer day into a brighter experience. Grab yours from April through July. Soak up warmer days under the summer sun or from the comfort of an air-conditioned room. Our Summer Ale works for wherever the hot days take you—and we won't judge you if you choose the latter.

MAKES 1 ALE-TAIL
SUMMER ALE MEZCAL "MARGARITA"

2 slices jalapeño chile
1 ripe strawberry, hulled
1½ ounces mezcal
¾ ounce fresh lime juice
½ ounce ginger simple syrup or plain simple syrup
3 ounces Samuel Adams Summer Ale
Lime wedge

In a cocktail shaker, muddle the jalapeño slices and strawberry. Add the mezcal, lime juice, and ginger simple syrup. Fill the shaker with ice and shake vigorously until well mixed.

Fill a highball glass with ice, then strain the mezcal mixture into the glass. Top with the Summer Ale. Garnish with a lime wedge and serve.

A hit for every occasion, this creamy BLT dip, which layers smoky bacon, ripe tomatoes, and crisp lettuce, is a deconstructed take on the timeless sandwich. **Melissa Wallace,** founder of **Sippin Snax,** a North Carolina–based artisanal bar-snack company, suggests serving this dip with the company's Beer Salted Pretzels, but potato chips and crudités are also great for dipping. Better yet, serve all three.

SMOKY **BLT DIP**

To cook the bacon, in a frying pan over medium-low heat, cook the bacon, turning as needed, until crisp, about 8 minutes. Transfer to paper towels to drain. Let cool.

To make the dip, in a serving bowl, combine the sour cream, mayonnaise, Worcestershire sauce, tomato powder, and pepper and mix well. Crumble the bacon into the mixture, then add the tomatoes and stir to mix. Top with the lettuce and arugula.

Serve at once with Beer Salted Pretzels for dipping.

8 ounces thick-cut bacon slices

2 cups sour cream or plain Greek yogurt

1 cup mayonnaise

1½ teaspoons Worcestershire sauce

½ teaspoon tomato powder

½ teaspoon ground white pepper

2 small Roma tomatoes, seeded and finely diced

1 cup shredded romaine lettuce hearts

½ cup chopped baby arugula

Sippin Snax Beer Salted Pretzels and/or Peppa Snax, potato chips, or crudités, for serving

This creamy classic is chock-full of fresh spinach, marinated artichoke hearts, and creamy cheeses. The secret to this particular recipe, which was created by entrepreneur and chef **Gary Hicks,** founder of **CookUp Catering** in Cincinnati, is the mix of ranch seasoning and Italian herbs. Easy to prepare and perfect for a crowd, it's at its best served warm straight from the oven, with plenty of dippers—and beer, of course—on hand.

SPINACH ARTICHOKE DIP

1 tablespoon olive oil, plus more for the baking dish

1 small yellow onion, finely chopped

2 garlic cloves, minced

1 pound spinach, stemmed and finely chopped

1 (6½-ounce) jar marinated artichoke hearts, drained and chopped

1 (8-ounce) package cream cheese, cut into pieces, at room temperature

1 cup sour cream

1 cup (about 4 ounces) shredded Italian cheese blend

¾ cup grated Parmesan cheese

1 (1-ounce) packet ranch seasoning, preferably Hidden Valley brand

2 teaspoons Italian herb seasoning

Pita chips or tortilla chips, for serving

Preheat the oven to 350°F. Oil a 9-inch square baking dish.

To cook the vegetables, in a large frying pan over medium heat, warm the oil. Add the onion and cook, stirring often, until softened, 5 to 7 minutes. Stir in the garlic and then add the spinach and cook, stirring, just until the spinach is wilted, about 1 minute. (If all the spinach won't fit at once, add it in batches, allowing each batch to wilt slightly before adding more.) Remove from the heat, drain off any liquid, and transfer to a large bowl.

To assemble the dip, add the artichoke hearts, cream cheese, sour cream, Italian cheese blend, ½ cup of the Parmesan, ranch seasoning, and 1 teaspoon of the herb seasoning to the spinach mixture and stir until well mixed and the cream cheese is smooth. Transfer to the prepared baking dish. Sprinkle the remaining ¼ cup Parmesan and 1 teaspoon herb seasoning evenly over the top.

Bake the dip, stirring once or twice, until heated through and bubbling, about 20 minutes. Serve warm with pita chips.

Created by nutritionist and wholesome food advocate **Sonal Khakhar,** founder of Massachusetts-based **Aahana's Naturals,** these savory vegan and gluten-free pancakes use sprouted mung beans as their base. Look for sprouted mung beans at well-stocked markets. Mung beans are a great source of protein, fiber, and essential minerals. They have anti-inflammatory properties and may even help lower cholesterol. Fresh ginger and jalapeño add loads of flavor and subtle heat. Serve these pancakes with your favorite chutney—we recommend peach or Major Grey's mango chutney for an extra-gingery kick.

MUNG BEAN PANCAKES WITH CHUTNEY

To make the batter, in a blender, combine the mung beans, yogurt, jalapeño, and ginger and blend on medium speed until a slightly coarse paste forms. Add the water, chickpea and rice flours, baking soda, and salt and blend on medium speed, stopping and scraping down the sides as needed, until a pancake-like batter forms, adding a little more water if needed for the correct consistency.

To cook the pancakes, heat a griddle or large frying pan over medium heat. When it is hot, lightly brush the surface with oil. For each pancake, ladle about ¼ cup of the batter onto the hot surface, spreading it into a round and being careful not to crowd the surface. Cook until the edges start to set, 2 to 3 minutes, then carefully flip the pancakes. Continue cooking until both sides are golden brown and the pancake is cooked through, about 2 minutes longer.

Serve warm with chutney.

1 cup sprouted mung beans

½ cup plant-based yogurt

1 small jalapeño chile, seeded, if desired, and finely chopped

½ teaspoon peeled and grated fresh ginger

1 cup water, plus more if needed

½ cup chickpea flour

½ cup rice flour

¼ teaspoon baking soda

1 teaspoon fine sea salt

Canola oil, for cooking

Chutney, for serving

Similar to samosas, sambuxas are Sudanese triangle-shaped stuffed pastries traditionally served to guests or at celebrations. The crisp, thin dough can encase both sweet and savory fillings. This recipe comes from **Gladys Shahtou**, founder of **Sambuxa NYC**, whose aim is to introduce Sudanese cuisine to the New York food scene. She has created the perfect vegetarian shareable with a delightful blend of creamy feta and fresh dill. Enjoy the "taste in the fold," and if you are in a hurry, use store-bought phyllo dough.

SAMBUXAS WITH FETA & DILL

To make the pastry, in a stand mixer fitted with the dough hook attachment, beat together 1 cup of the flour and the oil on low speed until well mixed. Add the remaining 1 cup flour and the warm water and continue to beat until a smooth dough forms. Cover the bowl with a kitchen towel, and let the dough rest at room temperature for 20 minutes. Gather the dough into a ball, wrap in plastic wrap, and refrigerate for 30 minutes.

Preheat the oven to 350°F. Line a large sheet pan with parchment paper.

To stretch the dough, cut it into 8 equal pieces and form each piece into a ball. Lightly dust a work surface with flour. Working with 1 dough ball at a time, and using a rolling pin, roll and stretch out the dough into a 6-inch round about ¹⁄₁₆-inch thick. Generously dust the dough round with flour. Repeat with the remaining dough balls, rolling them out, dusting them with flour, and then stacking them on top of one another as you work. When all the rounds are stacked, use the rolling pin to stretch the dough further to a 14-inch round.

Place the stacked dough rounds on the prepared sheet pan. Bake for 4 minutes, turning once halfway through. Transfer the stacked rounds to a wire rack and let cool completely. Reserve the sheet pan.

Cut the cooled stack of dough rounds vertically into 4 equal strips, each about 3½ inches wide. Cover the stack with a damp kitchen towel.

To make the filling, in a bowl, combine the feta, dill, and the pepper and coriander, if using, and mix well.

To fold each sambuxa, peel off a strip of dough and lay it on a work surface. Starting at one end of the strip, fold one edge over to form a triangle, then fold it over again to the opposite side to form a triangle, creating a pocket cone. Add about 1½ tablespoons of the filling into the pocket cone, then continue to fold the filled dough pocket from side to side, always forming a triangle, until you reach the end of the strip, tucking the end into the last fold. Repeat with the remaining dough strips and filling.

To bake the sambuxas, increase the oven temperature to 400°F. Arrange the sambuxas on the reserved sheet pan, spacing them evenly. Bake until golden brown, about 10 minutes. Transfer to a platter and serve at once.

Sambuxa Pastry

2 cups all-purpose flour, plus more for dusting

¼ cup canola or other neutral oil

½ cup warm water

Feta-Dill Filling

2 cups (about 8 ounces) crumbled feta cheese

½ cup finely chopped fresh dill

1 teaspoon ground white pepper (optional)

½ teaspoon ground coriander (optional)

Note: To use phyllo dough, cut the sheets lengthwise into strips 3½ inches wide; keep the strips covered to prevent drying. For each sambuxa, use 2 strips of dough, brushing each with a little neutral oil or melted and cooled ghee, before sandwiching the strips together, then folding and filling the strips as directed for the homemade dough.

PAMELA JONES, FOUNDER OF CHARBOY'S

CharBoy's was born out of the vision of Chicago native Pamela Jones, a veteran who served her country on active duty in both the US Army and US Navy. She's a trailblazer in the world of healthier marinades and sauce condiments, driven by a deep-rooted passion for food and a commitment to promoting better eating habits within families and communities.

Inspired by her own experiences with such family health issues as diabetes, high cholesterol, and high blood pressure, Pamela embarked on a mission to revolutionize the condiment industry. Collaborating with fellow food enthusiasts and professional chefs who shared her vision, she set out to create sauces and marinades, prioritizing quality ingredients and innovative recipes.

"I WOULD SAY TO ALL ENTREPRENEURS TO FOLLOW YOUR PASSION, EXPECT HARD WORK, AND NEVER GIVE UP! BREWING THE AMERICAN DREAM HAS BEEN INSTRUMENTAL IN HELPING OUR BUSINESS SUCCEED BY PROVIDING COACHING, MENTORING, RESOURCES, SUPPORT, AND ENDLESS OPPORTUNITIES FOR BRAND AWARENESS."

Pamela Jones

With relentless dedication, Pamela experimented with herbs, spices, and natural ingredients to develop products lower in sodium and sugar and free from chemical additives, without compromising on taste. That passion and inspiration led to the 2008 launch of CharBoy's, her Chicago-based company that continues to practice the small-batch craftmanship that marked its earliest years.

Today, CharBoy's sauces and marinades stand out for both their exceptional taste and their health-conscious approach. They're lower in sodium and sugar than many major brands, reflecting Pamela's unwavering commitment to the well-being of her customers. Through her entrepreneurial spirit and concern for the health of others, Pamela has created a trusted brand recognized for its positive impact on not only the condiment industry but also people's lives.

Makes 4 servings

A party and brewpub favorite, these marinated and grilled chicken wings, served with a simple but highly recommended dipping sauce, are elevated by the addition of **Pamela Jones's** Southern-style, Midwest-influenced barbecue sauce and marinade, each of which gets a healthy splash of Samuel Adams Boston Lager. Her sauces and marinades, which she sells through her company, **CharBoy's**, are health-conscious versions of decades-old family recipes. Whether you use whole wings or party wings, this shareable snack promises to be a crowd-pleaser at every family cookout, tailgate party, or other gathering.

CHICKEN WINGS WITH SMOKY BEER MARINADE

Dipping Sauce

1 cup CharBoy's BBQ Sauce or your favorite barbecue sauce

⅓ cup Samuel Adams Boston Lager

¼ teaspoon sweet paprika

¼ teaspoon granulated garlic

Wings

1 (1.16-ounce) packet CharBoy's Smoky Homestyle Marinade, mild or extra hot, or ⅓ cup of your favorite smoky chicken marinade

3 tablespoons Samuel Adams Boston Lager

2 tablespoons extra-virgin olive oil

2 pounds chicken wings, preferably party wings

To make the dipping sauce, in a small saucepan over medium heat, combine the barbecue sauce, beer, paprika, and garlic and bring to a simmer, stirring occasionally. Continue to simmer, stirring occasionally, until the flavors are blended and the sauce is slightly thickened, 5 to 7 minutes. Remove from the heat and set aside to cool.

To make the wings, in a large bowl, whisk together the marinade packet, beer, and oil. Add the chicken wings and, using your hands, rub the wings with the marinade, coating thoroughly and evenly. Cover and refrigerate for at least 15 minutes or up to 24 hours.

If grilling the wings, prepare a gas or charcoal grill for indirect cooking over medium heat (400°F). When the grill is ready, brush the grill grates clean. Add the chicken wings to the grill over indirect heat, close the grill lid, and cook, turning occasionally, until the wings are nicely browned and cooked through, about 20 minutes. Baste the wings with some of the sauce near the end of cooking.

If baking the wings, preheat the oven to 425°F. Arrange the wings in a single layer on a large sheet pan. Bake until the wings are nicely browned and cooked through, about 30 minutes. Baste the wings with some of the sauce near the end of cooking.

Serve the wings hot with the remaining sauce on the side for dipping.

Makes 4 servings

A beloved staple of Colombia and Venezuela, arepas de choclo, also called cachapas, are a delightful marriage of tender corn cakes and melty cheese. A blender pulls the ingredients together to create the perfect pancake batter, and a hot frying pan turns the batter into golden goodness. Chef **Isis Arrieta-Dennis,** owner of **The Arepa Place** in Cincinnati, recommends using P.A.N. Sweet Corn Mix to achieve the most authentic taste and texture. Enjoy these comforting arepas as a stand-alone treat, for breakfast or a snack, or paired with your favorite sides.

AREPAS DE CHOCLO

To make the arepas batter, in a blender, combine the corn mix, corn kernels, water, milk, butter, and salt and blend on medium speed until well mixed. Let stand until thickened, about 10 minutes.

To cook the arepas, preheat a frying pan over medium-low heat. Once the pan is hot, add 1 tablespon oil. When the oil is hot, ladle about ⅓ cup of the corn mixture into the frying pan, spreading it with the back of the ladle in a circle. Cook until the underside is golden brown, 5 to 7 minutes. Flip with a spatula and continue to cook until the second side is golden brown, about 5 minutes. Transfer to a plate and top with a slice of cheese. Fold them in half if you like. Keep warm. Repeat with the remaining batter and cheese, adding more oil as needed.

Serve the arepas warm. Arepas are typically served plain, but if you'd like a pop of color, garnish them with sliced avocado, cherry tomatoes, and/or cilantro.

1 cup P.A.N. Sweet Corn Mix

1 cup fresh or frozen corn kernels

1 cup water

½ cup whole milk

1 tablespoon unsalted butter, melted

¼ teaspoon fine sea salt

Canola or other neutral oil, for cooking

8 ounces queso fresco or other fresh white cheese, such as farmers' cheese, sliced

Sliced avocado, chopped cherry tomatoes, and/or chopped fresh cilantro, for garnish (optional)

★ BREWER'S FAVORITE ★

This recipe gives classic pizza dough a hoppy twist with the addition of Samuel Adams Boston Lager. Samuel Adams Brewer and Director of Partnerships **Jennifer Glanville Love** finds it's a perfect base for a barbecue-style pizza topped with Beer-Braised Pork with BBQ Sauce (page 140), or pulled pork or shredded chicken tossed with barbecue sauce. Red onion adds just the right amount of bite atop creamy mozzarella and nutty Parmesan. And, of course, you can't beat washing it all down with a cold Samuel Adams Boston Lager.

BBQ PIZZA WITH BRAISED PORK

3½ cups all-purpose flour, plus more as needed

1 envelope (2¼ teaspoons) instant dry yeast

1 tablespoon fine sea salt

1 tablespoon extra-virgin olive oil, plus more for greasing

1 (12-ounce) bottle Samuel Adams Boston Lager, warm (120°F)

½ cup favorite barbecue sauce

½ cup favorite pizza sauce

2 cups (about 8 ounces) loosely packed shredded whole-milk mozzarella cheese

½ cup diced red onion

1 cup braised, shredded pork or chicken

¼ cup (about 1 ounce) grated Parmesan cheese

To make the dough, in a large bowl, combine the flour, yeast, salt, and oil. Add the warm beer to the flour mixture, stirring with a fork until the dough is lumpy. Turn out the dough onto a floured work surface and knead until smooth and elastic, 5 to 8 minutes. The dough will start out a little sticky, so gradually add a little flour if needed to make it easier to handle. As you work with the dough, periodically poke it to see if it is ready. When it gently springs back after you poke it, you have finished kneading. The dough should weigh about 2 pounds. Divide it in half and form each half into a ball.

Lightly grease two 1-quart (or larger) airtight containers with oil. Put a dough ball into each container, cover tightly, and let the dough rise in a warm spot until doubled in size, 1 to 2 hours.

When ready to bake, position an oven rack in the bottom third of the oven and place a pizza stone on the rack. Preheat the oven to 500°F.

To stretch the dough, gently remove one dough ball from its container. Lightly grease a large pizza pan, sheet pan, or pizza screen with oil. On a lightly floured surface, stretch the dough into a round. For a thicker crust, stretch to a 12-inch round; for a thinner crust, stretch to 14 inches. Transfer the dough round to the pan.

To top the pizza, in a small bowl, stir together the barbecue sauce and pizza sauce. Spread half of the sauce mixture evenly on the pizza crust, leaving a ½-inch border. Evenly distribute half of the mozzarella, then half of the onion, and finally half of the braised pork over the sauce, keeping the ½-inch border free of toppings. Evenly sprinkle half of the Parmesan cheese over the top.

To bake the pizza, slide the pan onto the pizza stone and bake until the toppings are bubbling and the edge of the crust is golden brown, 10 to 15 minutes. Transfer to a cutting board and let rest for a few minutes before cutting into wedges to serve. Repeat with the remaining dough and toppings.

Makes 6 to 8 servings

This tahini loaf is an excellent example of how seeds can be a great alternative to grain in bread making. Its dense texture is perfect for slicing, toasting, and pairing with any sweet or savory spread. Enjoy this loaf at Passover when eating wheat, rye, and other grains is forbidden, or serve it as a gluten-free, dairy-free, low-carb, or keto option. This recipe comes from Israeli-born **Hila Krikov,** founder of **Sweet Tahini** in Needham, Massachusetts. Hila is committed to using nutritious pantry staples from the Middle East and Mediterranean in her company's artisanal plant-based products.

SEEDED TAHINI LOAF

Preheat the oven to 350°F. Lightly grease 9-inch loaf pan with oil or line the bottom and sides with parchment paper.

To make the dough, in a small bowl, stir together 6 tablespoons of the mixed seeds with the baking soda and salt. In a medium bowl, using an electric mixer, beat the eggs on medium-high speed until thick and fluffy, about 4 minutes. On low speed, add the tahini and date molasses and beat just until incorporated. Using a rubber spatula, fold in the seed mixture until well mixed. Pour the batter into the prepared pan and sprinkle the top with the remaining seeds.

Bake the bread until a toothpick inserted into the center comes out dry and the top is nicely browned, about 35 minutes. Let cool in the pan on a wire rack for 20 minutes, then turn out onto the rack, peel off the parchment, if using, turn upright, and let cool completely before serving.

Slice and serve with hummus, if desired. Store leftover bread in an airtight container at room temperature for up to 5 days, or slice and freeze for up to 6 months.

Canola or other neutral oil, for the loaf pan

½ cup mixed seeds, such as flaxseeds, white and black sesame seeds, sunflower seeds, and/or pumpkin seeds

1 teaspoon baking soda

½ teaspoon fine sea salt

4 large eggs

½ cup tahini

2 tablespoons date molasses, honey, or pure maple syrup

Hummus or other favorite spread, for serving (optional)

Empanadas—small turnovers popular in Latin America, Spain, and other countries—are a great portable feast and perfect for picnics, potlucks, tailgates, or simply sharing at home while watching a big game. **Pablo Mastandrea** is their number one fan and made it his mission to craft the perfect empanada. His quest resulted in **The Perfect Empanada,** where he serves up gourmet empanadas in Warren, Rhode Island. This Argentinian-style steak and mushroom version is enriched with Malbec wine, the country's most widely planted red grape variety. Baking instead of frying makes it a healthier option, plus it uses premade dough, making it a great recipe for beginners. Be sure to chill the filling before using to bring out the full richness of its flavors.

EMPANADAS WITH STEAK & MUSHROOMS

8 ounces beef sirloin tip steak

Fine sea salt

2 tablespoons olive oil

1 tablespoon unsalted butter

1½ red onions, finely chopped

8 ounces cremini or button mushrooms, stem ends trimmed, then thinly sliced

⅓ cup dry red wine, preferably Argentinian Malbec

2 (8-ounce) jars chimichurri sauce, divided

Freshly ground pepper

14 to 18 frozen empanada dough disks, about 5 inches in diameter

1 large egg yolk beaten with 2 teaspoons water, for egg wash

To cook the steak, season it all over with salt. Heat a large frying pan over medium-high heat and add 1 tablespoon of the oil. When the oil is hot, add the steak and sear, turning once, until well browned on both sides and cooked to medium-rare, 4 to 6 minutes. Transfer to a cutting board and let rest for 5 minutes. Cut the steak into ½-inch pieces and set aside.

To make the filling, in the same pan over medium-high heat, melt the butter with the remaining 1 tablespoon oil. Add the onions and mushrooms and cook, stirring occasionally, until softened, 6 to 8 minutes. Return the steak to the pan, stir to combine, and increase the heat to high. Cook, stirring, until well mixed, 2 to 3 minutes.

Pour in the wine and cook, stirring to scrape up any browned bits from the pan bottom, for 3 to 4 minutes to simmer off the alcohol. Remove the pan from the heat and stir in 1 jar of the chimichurri sauce. Let sit for 5 minutes. Season with salt and pepper, transfer to a bowl, let cool, cover, and refrigerate for at least 1 hour or up to 12 hours before assembling the empanadas.

Preheat the oven to 425°F. Line a large sheet pan with parchment paper.

To assemble the empanadas, lay out the empanada dough disks on a work surface. Divide the chilled filling evenly among the disks, spooning it in the center of each disk (about 1 tablespoon per empanada). Brush the edge on half of each disk with the egg wash, then fold over the disk to form a half-moon. Using your fingers, press the edges together firmly, then, using a fork, crimp the edges. Arrange the empanadas on the prepared sheet pan and brush the tops with the remaining egg wash.

Bake the empanadas until golden brown, 10 to 15 minutes. (An instant-read thermometer inserted into the center should register 165°F.) Let cool in the pan on a wire rack for 10 minutes, then serve warm with the remaining chimichurri sauce for dipping.

These crisp, golden brown, pizza-inspired egg rolls are filled with a rich cheese sauce, spicy Italian sausage, and pepperoni and make a perfect addition to game night or any casual get-together. They are a favorite of the Samuel Adams Boston Taproom brewmaster, especially when paired with a pint of Samuel Adams Summer Ale. This great snack was created by Chicago native **Nikkita Randle,** founder of **Twisted Eggroll,** who strives to cultivate a fresh experience by adding a unique twist to traditional recipes. Using purchased egg roll wrappers means these savory bites come together in a snap.

PIZZA EGGROLLS

To make the cheese sauce, in a saucepan over medium-low heat, melt the butter. Whisk in the flour and 1 teaspoon salt until smooth. Slowly whisk in the milk and bring the mixture to a simmer while whisking constantly. Stir in the mozzarella, provolone, and Parmesan cheeses and continue to stir until the cheeses are melted and the sauce is smooth and slightly thickened, about 5 minutes. Taste and season with salt and pepper. Remove from the heat and let cool slightly.

To make the sausage meatballs, divide the sausage into 24 equal portions and roll each portion into a ball. Line a plate with paper towel and set it near the stove. In a large frying pan over medium heat, warm the olive oil. Add the sausage balls and cook, turning occasionally, until browned on all sides, about 5 minutes. Using a slotted spoon, transfer to the paper towel–lined plate to drain and cool slightly.

To assemble the eggrolls, on a clean work surface, position an egg roll wrapper with one point toward you. Place 2 tablespoons of the cheese sauce, 2 pepperoni slices, and 3 sausage balls in the center of the wrapper. Fold the bottom point up over the filling, then fold the sides in toward the center over the filling, overlapping the edges. Roll up the egg roll toward the remaining point. Moisten the top corner with the beaten egg and press to seal. Repeat with the remaining wrappers and filling ingredients. Brush the eggrolls lightly with the beaten egg.

To fry the eggrolls, in a deep, wide saucepan, pour peanut oil to a depth of 2 inches. Heat to 375°F on a deep-frying thermometer. Working in batches as needed to avoid crowding, fry the egg rolls, turning a few times with tongs, until golden brown on all sides, about 2 minutes. Transfer to paper towels to drain. Serve warm, accompanied with marinara sauce for dipping, if desired.

Cheese Sauce

1 tablespoon unsalted butter

2 tablespoons all-purpose flour

Fine sea salt and freshly ground pepper

1 cup whole milk

½ cup shredded mozzarella cheese

½ cup shredded provolone cheese

½ cup grated Parmesan cheese

Eggrolls

1 pound spicy Italian sausages, casings removed

2 tablespoons olive oil

8 egg roll wrappers, about 6½ inches square

8 ounces sliced pepperoni (16 slices)

1 large egg, lightly beaten with 1 teaspoon water

Peanut oil, for frying

Marinara sauce, warmed, for dipping (optional)

★ BREWER'S FAVORITE ★

Shrimp poached in beer is a timeless classic, offering a unique twist to the traditional shrimp cocktail. The beer infuses the shrimp with subtle flavors, enhancing their natural sweetness. Serve at room temperature or chilled with zesty cocktail sauce for a refreshing appetizer that never fails to impress, and is perfect for any occasion year-round.

BEER-POACHED **SHRIMP COCKTAIL**

2 (12-ounce) bottles Samuel Adams Boston Lager or Summer Ale

2 cups water

1 whole head garlic, unpeeled

¼ cup pickling spice

2 bay leaves

6 drops Tabasco sauce

2 pounds large shrimp in the shell

Cocktail sauce, for serving

To make the poaching liquid, in a 6-quart stockpot, combine the beer, water, garlic head, pickling spice, bay leaves, and Tabasco sauce and bring to a boil over medium-high heat, and boil for 10 minutes.

To poach the shrimp, reduce the heat to medium-low and add the shrimp to the liquid. Poach the shrimp until they are pink and firm, about 5 minutes. Drain the shrimp, transfer them to a bowl, and let cool to room temperature.

Serve the shrimp at room temperature or cover and refrigerate and serve chilled, accompanied with cocktail sauce.

★ BREWER'S FAVORITE ★

These irresistible crab fritters combine lump crabmeat, sweet corn kernels, and fresh chives and parsley, all coated in a crispy beer batter made with Samuel Adams Boston Lager. Each bite harmonizes sweet, savory, and hoppy flavors. Serve hot with spicy rémoulade or a lemon aioli for a satisfying appetizer or main dish.

CRAB FRITTERS WITH BOSTON LAGER

To make the beer batter, in a medium bowl, sift together the flour, baking powder, salt, and nutmeg. In a large bowl, combine the beer, chives, parsley, chile (if using), and onion and stir to mix well. Add the flour mixture to the beer mixture and stir just until blended.

Add the crabmeat, corn kernels, and Tabasco and, using a rubber spatula, fold in gently. In a small bowl, whisk the egg white until stiff peaks form. Using the rubber spatula, gently fold the egg white into the batter.

To fry the fritters, line a large plate with paper towels and set it near the stove. Pour oil to a depth of ¼ inch into a large, heavy frying pan and heat over medium-high heat. When the oil is hot, carefully add 2 tablespoons of the batter into the pan for each fritter, spacing the fritters at least 1 inch apart to avoid crowding the pan. Fry, turning once or twice, until cooked through and golden brown, about 5 minutes. Transfer to the paper towel–lined plate to drain. Repeat with the remaining batter. Serve at once.

¾ cup all-purpose flour

1 teaspoon baking powder

1¼ teaspoons kosher salt

¼ teaspoon freshly grated nutmeg

¾ cup Samuel Adams Boston Lager or Summer Ale

¼ cup finely chopped fresh chives

2 tablespoons finely chopped fresh flat-leaf parsley

1 serrano or jalapeño chile, seeded and minced (optional)

1 teaspoon grated yellow onion

¾ cup fresh-cooked lump crabmeat, picked over for shell fragments

1¼ cups fresh or frozen corn kernels

1 to 2 dashes Tabasco sauce

1 large egg white

Canola oil, for frying

A pan of warm focaccia not only fills your kitchen with enticing aromas but is also satisfying to make. This versatile bread recipe comes from **Axel Erkenswick,** chef and cofounder of **Smack Dab Chicago,** who also likes to top it with shredded cheese or chopped fresh herbs just before baking. However you top it, it makes a great snack or addition to an alfresco picnic with plenty of cold beer. The citrus wheat Samuel Adams Summer Ale in the dough gives a tangy boost to the flavor. Fun fact: The Founding Fathers called beer "liquid bread" and refused to tax it!

FOCACCIA WITH SUMMER ALE

Poolish Pre-ferment

5 cups (650 grams) bread flour

2 (12-ounce) bottles Samuel Adams Summer Ale or citrus wheat ale, at room temperature

1 teaspoon instant dry yeast

Main Dough

2²/₃ cups (350 grams) bread flour

1 tablespoon fine sea salt

9 tablespoons extra-virgin olive oil

Coarse sea salt, for sprinkling

To make the poolish, in a very large bowl or other food-grade container, stir together the flour, beer, and yeast until the flour is evenly moistened. Cover and set aside at room temperature until the mixture triples in volume and becomes very bubbly, about 10 hours. At this point, the poolish can be refrigerated for 1 to 2 days; bring to room temperature before proceeding.

To make the main dough, add the flour, fine sea salt, and 3 tablespoons of the oil to the poolish and stir to mix well. Knead the dough until it is elastic, slightly smooth, and holds a ball shape, 8 to 10 minutes. Flip the dough over and fold each of the four corners into the middle to stretch each side. (Think of how you close a cardboard box: the sides close first and then the top and bottom close.) While holding the tension from the four folds with one of your hands, flip the dough back over, and gravity will hold the seam in the bowl. Now it should look like a dough ball.

Cover the bowl with a damp kitchen towel and let the dough rest for 30 minutes. Repeat the flipping, folding, and the 30-minute rest and then repeat a third time for a total 1½ hours resting time.

To form the focaccia, grease a large rimmed sheet pan with 3 tablespoons of the oil. When the dough has rested for the third and final time, transfer it to the oiled sheet pan and drizzle with 1 tablespoon of the oil. Press and stretch the dough out with your hands into a rectangle that nearly fills the sheet pan. If dough resists stretching, let it rest for 5 minutes between stretches until it fills the pan. Cover loosely with plastic wrap and set aside at room temperature until the dough is puffed and fills the pan, 2 to 3 hours.

Preheat the oven to 475°F. Drizzle the remaining 2 tablespoons olive oil over the top of the dough. Using your fingers, quickly and gently dimple the dough from one edge to the other. You'll be slightly spreading the dough, but do not deflate it completely. Sprinkle coarse sea salt evenly over the top.

Bake the focaccia until golden brown, about 15 minutes. Let cool completely in the pan on a wire rack before cutting to serve. The focaccia is best the day it is made, but leftovers will keep in an airtight container at room temperature for up to 3 days; if stored, rewarm or toast the bread before using.

Refreshingly updated, this cocktail combines probiotic-rich ginger-lime kombucha and a splash of Goslings Rum. **Emily Sheridan,** founder of Rhode Island–based **Fieldstone Kombucha,** uses organic ingredients and a meticulous fermentation process to produce her beverage, which she labels "spicy ginger" and describes as "a healthy take on ginger ale." Kombucha is increasingly popular due to its possible health benefits, from boosting the immune system and aiding digestion to ridding the body of toxins, and Emily is convinced that "sitting on the back porch at the end of the day with a kombucha cocktail always helps!"

DARK & STORMY
WITH GINGER-LIME KOMBUCHA

To make the cocktail, fill a highball glass with ice. Add the rum and lime juice and stir to combine. Pour in the kombucha, garnish with the lime wedge, and serve.

2 ounces dark rum, preferably Goslings Rum

Squeeze of fresh lime juice

5 ounces Fieldstone Kombucha Farm Dreams Spicy Ginger or other craft ginger-lime or ginger kombucha

Lime wedge or wheel, for garnish

Create the perfect summer vibe with this refreshing drink that combines crisp, citrusy Samuel Adams Summer Ale with zesty lemonade from **Little Maven Lemonade** in Rhode Island. Little Maven founder **Mariana Silva Buck** began producing lemonade flavors from all over the world after her daughter's request to set up a lemonade stand to make some pocket money. This easy-sipping drink is perfect for outdoor get-togethers when the temperatures soar.

CITRUS BERRY REFRESHER
WITH SUMMER ALE

1 ounce raspberry vodka

2 ounces lemonade, preferably Little Maven Lemonade

6 ounces Samuel Adams Summer Ale or citrus wheat ale

Lemon wedge or wheel, for garnish

To make the cocktail, fill a pint glass with ice. Add the vodka and lemonade and stir to combine. Pour in the ale, garnish with the lemon wedge, and serve.

Makes 1 cocktail

★ BREWER'S FAVORITE ★

With its golden hues and refreshing zest, this harmonious blend of gin, tangy citrus notes, and the crisp, effervescent flavor of Samuel Adams Summer Ale embodies the warmth of a sunset. Sip away as the flavors dance on your palate, inviting pure relaxation.

SUMMER ALE **SUNSET**

To make the cocktail, fill a pint glass with ice. Add the gin, grapefruit juice, and lime juice. Stir with a bar spoon until combined. Pour the ale over the ice and garnish with the lime. Serve.

1 ounce gin

1 ounce grapefruit juice

¼ ounce fresh lime juice

6 ounces Samuel Adams Summer Ale or citrus wheat ale

Lime wedge or wheel, for garnish

LEGENDARY
LUNCHES

Lift your salad greens from every day to extraordinary by pairing them with a sweet, tangy, spicy vinaigrette. Jamaican-born **Kamaal Jarrett,** owner of **Hillside Harvest** in Boston, had plenty of fun elevating this crunchy romaine, cucumber, and herbs salad with his blend of lime, honey, and a bold kick of his signature hot sauce. Add some grilled chicken or sliced steak plus a crisp beer and you have a memorable lunch.

BIG GREEN SALAD
WITH HOT PEPPER VINAIGRETTE

To make the vinaigrette, in a large bowl, whisk together the oil, hot sauce, honey, and lime zest and juice until smooth. Season with salt and pepper.

To finish the salad, add the lettuce, cucumbers, mint, and basil to the bowl that holds the dressing. Using your hands or a pair of tongs, toss everything together until the leaves are evenly glazed with the vinaigrette. Serve at once.

3 tablespoons olive oil

2 tablespoons Hillside Harvest Original Hot Pepper Hot Sauce or hot sauce of your choice

1 teaspoon honey

Finely grated zest and juice of 1 lime

Fine sea salt and freshly ground pepper

1 head romaine lettuce, cored and chopped

1 large or two small cucumbers, thinly sliced

½ cup chopped fresh mint leaves

½ cup chopped fresh basil leaves

Makes 4 to 6 servings

This recipe comes from **Gladys Shahtou,** founder of **Sambuxa NYC.** In her homeland of Sudan, this vegetable salad with a rich, creamy peanut dressing is served with every meal to temper the fieriness of the country's traditional dishes, and variations on the salad are found on tables in many other African countries. Rich in protein and healthy fats, it makes a satisfying light meal with some pita bread or can be a welcome side for spicy meat dishes. Either way, a chilled Samuel Adams Wicked Easy is the ideal partner. If you want to dress up the salad a bit, Gladys suggests adding a handful of arugula, some chopped carrots, or even a dollop of plain yogurt.

SALATA DAKWA

4 Roma tomatoes, halved, seeded, and cut into ½-inch pieces

1 English cucumber, cut into ½-inch pieces

1 bunch scallions, white and green parts, finely chopped

1 cup (about 4 ounces) crumbled feta cheese

2 tablespoons toasted sesame oil

2 tablespoons creamy peanut butter

2 tablespoons warm water

2 tablespoons fresh lemon juice

1 teaspoon ground cumin

½ teaspoon fine sea salt

½ teaspoon freshly ground pepper

Pita bread, warmed, for serving

To assemble the salad, in a large, shallow serving bowl, toss together the tomatoes, cucumber, scallions, and feta. Drizzle the sesame oil over the top and toss gently to coat evenly.

To make the dressing, in a small bowl, whisk together the peanut butter and water until smooth. Add the lemon juice, cumin, salt, and pepper and whisk until well mixed.

To serve, pour the peanut butter dressing over the tomato mixture and toss gently to coat evenly. Serve at once with pita bread.

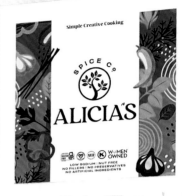

BREWING THE
AMERICAN DREAM
Winner

SOUPS · DIPS · MARINADES · MORE

simple
versatile
cooking

"We achieve great flavors by
letting quality, all natural,
simple ingredients shine through.
Enjoy & Happy Cooking!"

- Alicia Haddad - Founder

LOW SODIUM | NUT FREE | NO FILLERS
NO PRESERVATIVES | NO ARTIFICIAL INGREDIENTS

CERTIFIED GLUTEN FREE · VEGAN · KETO CERTIFIED · K · WOMEN OWNED

ALICIA HADDAD, FOUNDER OF ALICIA'S SPICE CO.

From the moment she could stand on a stool and hold a spoon, Alicia Haddad explored the world of recipe experimentation. Guided by her grandmother Leta, Alicia learned the significance of growing vegetables, cooking, baking, and canning. These early years in the kitchen not only cultivated a deep appreciation for family bonds and for the importance of preparing simple, healthy meals but also ultimately led to the launch of Alicia's Spice Co.

Throughout her journey, Alicia had numerous allergic reactions and underwent the arduous process of identifying intolerances to various food components, such as gluten, sodium, dyes, anticaking agents, and artificial ingredients. Faced with the challenge of finding flavorful foods and spice blends that met her dietary restrictions, she recognized a gap in the market for healthy, allergen-friendly seasoning blends. Motivated to address this gap, she established Alicia's Spice Co. in Worcester, Massachusetts, in 2015, offering simple, flavorful, and allergen-safe cooking solutions that everyone can enjoy. Today, Alicia's Spice Co., which remains woman owned and operated, prides itself on being an all-natural, certified gluten-free, vegan, kosher, keto, and low-sodium manufacturer of seasoning blends.

When she is not busy running her very successful company, Alicia actively engages with various communities in central Massachusetts, often serving as a guest speaker in undergraduate classes in local colleges. She dedicates her time to mentoring young entrepreneurs and contributes to food pantries, shelters, and similar people-oriented organizations. Alicia's commitment to giving back reflects her belief in the importance of supporting others whenever possible.

"BREWING THE AMERICAN DREAM MEANS FAMILY! WHEN YOU HAVE A TEAM OF MENTORS—TRUE ENTREPRENEURS WHO UNDERSTAND THE JOURNEY AND PROCESS, WHO BELIEVE IN YOUR MISSION, AND DREAM AS YOU DO, WHO TEACH YOU, GUIDE YOU, ENCOURAGE YOU, SUPPORT YOU WHEN NEEDED—THAT IS THE TRUE DEFINITION OF BREWING THE AMERICAN DREAM."

Alicia Haddad

In 2021, Alicia received an award in recognition of her achievements from Brewing the American Dream's Pitch Room. Grateful for the acknowledgment, Alicia describes Brewing the American Dream as a supportive family of mentors and fellow entrepreneurs who understand the journey and the process. Their steadfast belief in her mission and dream has been instrumental in her success.

Reflecting on her entrepreneurial journey, Alicia offers valuable advice to fellow entrepreneurs: never give up on your dreams, and never accept no for an answer. With perseverance, resilience, and support from mentors, success is within reach.

A family favorite for dinners and gatherings, this recipe has held a special place in **Alicia Haddad's** heart since childhood. The addition of the simple yet versatile Garlic Chive Seasoning blend from her company **Alicia's Spice Co.** adds a burst of flavor to marinated steak served over crisp lettuce, ripe tomatoes, and chives. Want a heartier meal? Serve the steak with grilled corn and garlic bread (hint: Try the seasoning on the bread!). The seasoning can also be used on grilled or stir-fried chicken, pork, or vegetables.

SALAD WITH GARLIC-CHIVE STEAK BITES

Marinated Steak Bites

2 tablespoons red wine vinegar

2 tablespoons water

1½ tablespoons Alicia's Spice Co. Garlic Chive Seasoning Blend, or other garlic-onion seasoning salt mixed with ½ teaspoon black pepper

1½ tablespoons extra-virgin olive oil

2 teaspoons firmly packed dark brown sugar

1½ pounds boneless sirloin steak, cut into 1½-inch pieces

Salad

¼ cup extra-virgin olive oil

2 tablespoons red wine vinegar

1 teaspoon Dijon mustard

Fine sea salt and freshly ground pepper

1 large head red or green leaf lettuce, cored and chopped

1 large, ripe heirloom tomato, cored and chopped

Chopped fresh chives, for garnish

Crusty bread, for serving

To marinate the steak bites, in a bowl, whisk together the vinegar, water, seasoning blend, oil, and sugar, mixing well. Add the steak pieces and turn to coat. Cover the bowl and refrigerate for at least 2 hours or up to 8 hours.

If using bamboo skewers, soak in water to cover for 30 minutes. Prepare a gas or charcoal grill for direct cooking over medium heat (400°F).

To assemble the skewers, while the grill heats, remove the steak pieces from the marinade and pat dry with paper towels. Thread the steak pieces onto skewers.

To grill the steak skewers, when the grill is ready, brush the grill grates clean. Add the skewers to the grill over direct heat, close the grill lid, and cook, turning occasionally to brown on all sides, until cooked to your liking, about 10 minutes for medium-rare. Transfer the skewers to a plate and let rest for about 10 minutes. Make the vinaigrette and salad while the steak rests.

To make the vinaigrette, in a jar with a lid, combine the oil, vinegar, mustard, and a pinch each of salt and pepper, cap tightly, and shake well.

To assemble the salad, add the lettuce to a bowl, drizzle with the vinaigrette, and toss to coat. Divide the lettuce evenly among four plates. Top the lettuce with the tomato, dividing it evenly. Slide the steak pieces from the skewers and arrange on top of the salad. Garnish with chives and serve at once, with bread alongside.

This colorful salad captures the spirit of Portugal's sunny culinary charm. It's ideal for picnics or would be great paired with a cheese board. The recipe comes from **Rodrigo Vargas,** owner of **American Vinegar Works,** who warns against overcooking the carrots. You should be able to spear them with a fork without them turning to mush. The subtle spiciness of the sweet paprika balances the light sourness of his Better Than Champagne Chardonnay Wine Vinegar and the sweetness of the carrots. According to Rodrigo, you are not going for "sauce." The liquid should be just enough to soak into the carrots and leave them wet, not drowning.

ALGARVE **CARROT SALAD**

1 bunch carrots (about 1 lb), peeled and cut into ¼-inch-thick rounds

3 tablespoons white wine vinegar, preferably American Vinegar Works Better Than Champagne Chardonnay Wine Vinegar

¼ teaspoon sweet paprika

1½ tablespoons extra-virgin olive oil

1 large bay leaf, halved

1 garlic clove, very thinly sliced

2 to 3 tablespoons roughly chopped fresh flat-leaf parsley

Fine sea salt

To par-cook the carrots, bring a saucepan two-thirds full of salted water to a boil over high heat. Add the carrots and cook, stirring a few times, until crisp-tender, about 5 minutes. Drain well and add to a deep, narrow bowl.

To marinate the carrots, in a small bowl, whisk together the vinegar and paprika, then whisk in the oil. Pour over the still-warm carrots, add the bay leaf, garlic, and parsley, and season with salt. Stir together gently, then set aside at room temperature for at least 1½ hours or up to 2½ hours, stirring occasionally.

To finish the salad, after the carrots have rested, taste and adjust the seasoning with salt and vinegar if needed. Remove and discard the bay leaf, then serve. The salad can be prepared up to 1 day in advance and stored in an airtight container in the refrigerator. Bring to room temperature before serving.

Championed for its health benefits and appreciated for its unique texture, nopal cactus contributes a nutritious boost to this salad, blending seamlessly with the vibrant flavors of tomato, onion, and cilantro. Suitable for lunch or a light dinner, this authentic Mexican salad is shared by mother and daughter **Julie and Bessie King,** owners of **Villa México Café** in Boston. For a heartier meal, top the salad with grilled chicken or fish.

CACTUS SALAD

To prepare the nopales, rinse in a fine-mesh sieve under cold running water, then drain well. You can leave the nopales in long strips or chop the strips into small pieces.

To assemble the salad, in a serving bowl, toss together the nopales, tomato, onion, and cilantro. In a small bowl, whisk together the oil, lime juice, oregano, and salt. Pour the lime dressing over the nopales mixture and toss gently. Cover and refrigerate for at least 1 hour or up to overnight.

To serve, garnish with a scattering of cheese and serve chilled.

2 cups drained jarred or canned nopales

1 large ripe tomato, finely chopped

1 small white onion, finely chopped

¼ cup finely chopped fresh cilantro leaves and stems

2 tablespoons olive oil

2 tablespoons fresh lime juice

1 teaspoon dried oregano

½ teaspoon fine sea salt

Crumbled queso fresco, for garnish

Take a trip to the Caribbean with this refreshingly different pasta salad from chef **Shelly Flash** of New York City's **2 Girls & a Cookshop.** Your macaroni will get an upgrade with the addition of crisp carrots, fragrant red onion, and bright scallions tossed in a creamy and sweet dressing with a slight kick of cayenne. With this recipe, chef Shelly, whose cooking is inspired by the vibrant cookshops of Jamaica and the melting pot of New York City, has brought a piece of her Jamaican childhood—and a delightful culinary twist on a classic— to your table. From chain eateries to humble cookshops on the side of a country road, macaroni salad is a beloved side dish throughout the island of Jamaica and is often served alongside crispy fried chicken. It perfectly completes any comfort meal.

CARIBBEAN **MAC SALAD**

Dressing

½ cup mayonnaise

½ can (7 ounces) sweetened condensed milk

¼ cup apple cider vinegar

1 teaspoon sweet paprika

1 teaspoon granulated garlic

1 teaspoon yellow mustard powder

1 teaspoon cayenne pepper

Fine sea salt and freshly ground black pepper

Mac Salad

Fine sea salt

8 ounces elbow macaroni

¼ cup peeled, finely chopped carrot

½ red onion, finely chopped (about ¼ cup)

4 scallions, green parts only, thinly sliced

To make the dressing, in a bowl, whisk together the mayonnaise, condensed milk, vinegar, paprika, garlic, mustard powder, and cayenne until smooth. Season with salt and black pepper. Cover and refrigerate until ready to serve.

To cook the macaroni, bring a large pot two-thirds full of salted water to a boil over high heat. Add the macaroni and cook, stirring occasionally, until al dente, according to the package directions. Drain into a colander and rinse well under cold running water. Let cool completely.

To assemble the mac salad, in a large bowl, combine the macaroni, carrot, red onion, and half of the scallions. Pour the dressing over the pasta mixture and toss to coat evenly. Cover and refrigerate for at least 1 hour or up to overnight before serving. The salad will thicken as it sits in the refrigerator, so be sure to stir well before serving.

Serve the salad chilled, garnished with the remaining scallions.

SAMUEL ADAMS
COLD SNAP

You've waited for months, and finally brighter days are so close you can taste them. The fleeting moment of spring soon to be chased away by summer is captured flawlessly in Cold Snap, a hazy white ale with a squeeze of citrus and a blend of ten fruits and spices. Like spring, it's here for a limited time, from January through March. Toast to hoping for Punxsutawney Phil's call for an early spring, spring sports madness, the inevitable arrival of spring cleaning, or your best try at New Year's resolutions. Cold Snap will prove a seamless addition no matter the occasion.

MAKES 1 ALE-TAIL
COLD SNAP BEE'S KNEES

2 ounces gin
½ ounce fresh lemon juice
½ ounce honey simple syrup
¼ ounce ginger liqueur, such as
Barrow's Intense
3 ounces Samuel Adams Cold Snap
1 star anise
1 piece candied ginger, speared with
a cocktail pick

In a cocktail shaker, combine the gin, lemon juice, honey simple syrup, and ginger liqueur. Fill the shaker with ice and shake vigorously until well mixed.

Strain into a coupe glass. Top with the Cold Snap. Garnish with the star anise and candied ginger and serve.

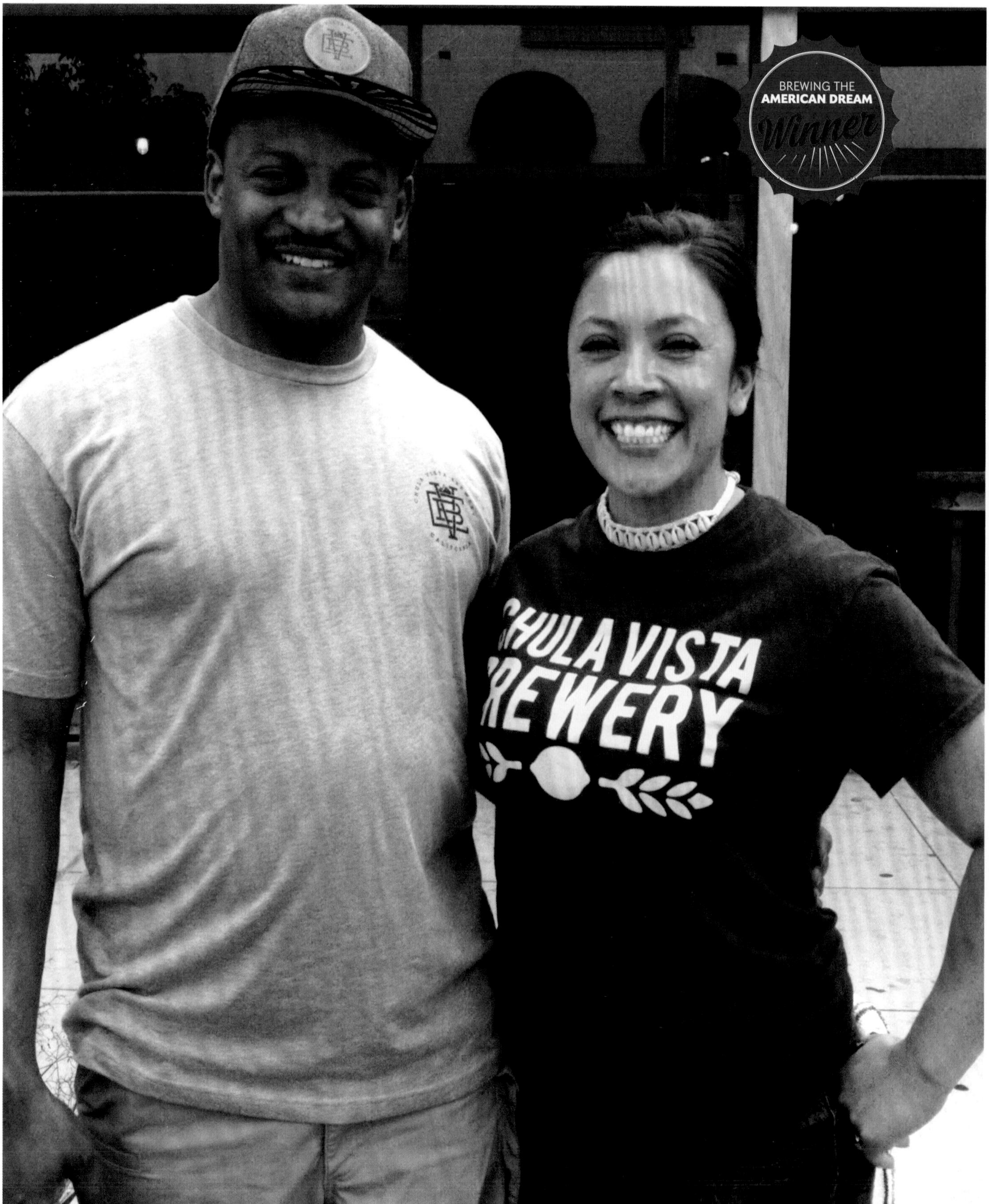
BREWING THE
AMERICAN DREAM
Winner

TIMOTHY JAMES PARKER, FOUNDER OF CHULA VISTA BREWERY

Timothy Parker's journey originated in the bustling city of Chicago, where his culinary passion took root at the tender age of six. His formative years were spent eagerly assisting his mother in the kitchen, honing his skills, and fearlessly experimenting with various recipes. Despite initial reluctance from family members, Timothy's dogged pursuit and culinary prowess earned him the title of family chef, a role he embraced with enthusiasm and dedication.

At eighteen, Timothy embarked on a new chapter, enlisting in the US Navy. Stationed in San Diego, California, he served as a search and rescue swimmer for over two decades. It was during his naval career that Timothy's affinity for craft beer blossomed. A pivotal moment occurred at a San Diego Padres baseball game when, under orders from his commanding officer, Timothy sampled Samuel Adams Boston Lager—a moment that marked the beginning of his love affair with craft beer. To this day, Samuel Adams Cherry Wheat remains a personal favorite. Throughout his deployments around the globe, Timothy made it his mission to seek out exceptional beers, fueling his interest in craft beer. This passion was heightened when a friend introduced him to the art of homebrewing, reigniting his creativity and rekindling his fervor for craft.

As his navy career approached its midpoint, Timothy found himself contemplating his post-military path. Following a reflective run in 2015, the idea of opening a brewery in his beloved neighborhood of Chula Vista began to take shape. Despite the saturated brewery scene in San Diego, Chula Vista lacked a brewing presence, motivating Timothy to fill that void. With the decision

> "I'VE PURSUED MY DREAMS WITH DETERMINATION, AND WHILE NOT EVERY ENDEAVOR HAS SUCCEEDED, THE BREWERY HAS THRIVED AS A TESTAMENT TO PERSEVERANCE AND PASSION. ALWAYS WORK TO MAKE YOUR THOUGHTS AND DREAMS A REALITY."

Timothy James Parker

made, he and his wife, Dali Parker, embarked on this entrepreneurial journey, opening their inaugural brewery in downtown Chula Vista in 2017.

Despite facing a series of deployments shortly after the brewery's launch, Timothy seized the opportunity to participate and ultimately triumph in the Brewing the American Dream Brewer Experienceship competition in 2018. Upon returning home from a deployment, he was flown out to Boston, where he received invaluable guidance from the team at Samuel Adams—an experience that served as a catalyst for his and Dali's burgeoning venture.

In 2019, Timothy made the pivotal decision to retire from the navy, prioritizing quality time with his family. By 2021, the brewery was flourishing and had expanded to a second location. Throughout his life, Timothy has pursued his dreams with steadfast determination, understanding that not every endeavor will yield success. Today, Chula Vista Brewery stands as a testament to the power of perseverance and passion, a beacon of inspiration for those who dare to transform their aspirations into reality.

This vegan version of a traditional French onion soup comes from brewer **Timothy James Parker** of **Chula Vista Brewery** in San Diego County, California. His secret ingredient is the hoppy flavor of his West Coast IPA paired with sweet caramelized onions and good-quality vegetable broth. You don't actually taste the beer in the finished soup, but the depth of flavor and robustness it imparts give this hearty dish a noticeable wow factor. To make a nonvegan version of this recipe, use chicken or beef broth instead of vegetable broth and dairy-based Cheddar or Gruyère to top the toasts.

VEGAN ONION SOUP WITH BEER

¼ cup olive oil, plus more for brushing

3 large yellow onions, thinly sliced (6 to 8 cups)

Fine sea salt and freshly ground pepper

6 cups vegetable broth

2 (12-ounce) bottles Chula Vista Xela West Coast IPA or Warplanes Hazy Pale Ale or your favorite IPA

2 bay leaves

¼ teaspoon dried thyme

Pinch of ground allspice

12 to 16 baguette slices, cut on the diagonal

2 cups (about 8 ounces) shredded vegan cheese, such as dairy-free Cheddar or Swiss

1 tablespoon apple cider vinegar, or more to taste

To caramelize the onions, in a large soup pot over medium-high heat, warm the oil. Add the onions, season with salt and pepper, and stir to combine. Cover the pot, reduce the heat to low, and cook, stirring occasionally, until the onions are caramelized, about 40 minutes.

To prepare the soup, add the broth, beer, bay leaves, thyme, allspice, 1 teaspoon salt, and 1 teaspoon pepper, increase the heat to medium-high, and bring to a boil. Reduce the heat to medium-low and simmer until the onions are quite soft and the broth has a nice onion flavor, about 30 minutes.

To make the cheese toasts, preheat the oven to 400°F. Lightly brush the baguette slices on both sides with oil and arrange in a single layer on a sheet pan. Place in the oven and toast, turning once, until light golden brown on both sides, about 4 minutes. Remove from the oven, top the toasts with the cheese, dividing it evenly, and return the pan to the oven. Bake until the cheese has melted, about 5 minutes, then remove from the oven.

To finish the soup, stir in the vinegar and season with a pinch each of salt and pepper. Taste and adjust the seasoning with more salt, pepper, and vinegar if needed.

To serve, ladle the soup into bowls and top each serving with 2 cheese-topped toasts.

This cheery, vegan-friendly soup was shared by **Farmer Foodie** founder **Alison Elliott,** whose company mantra is "people, planet, product." The wow factor comes from roasting the carrots, which enriches the flavor and texture of the soup. Alison adds a generous sprinkle of Farmer Foodie's Golden Chedda Cashew Parm plus plenty of ginger and miso to the soup pot. The showstopping touch is the crunchy spiced chickpea garnish.

CARROT SOUP WITH CRISPY CHICKPEAS

Carrot Soup

2 pounds carrots, scrubbed or peeled, and quartered

1 sweet white onion, quartered

3 tablespoons extra-virgin olive oil

Fine sea salt and freshly ground black pepper

3 garlic cloves, grated

2-inch piece fresh ginger, peeled and grated

½ small serrano chile, seeded if desired and finely chopped

5 cups vegetable broth

3 tablespoons miso paste

2 tablespoons Farmer Foodie Golden Chedda Cashew Parm or nutritional yeast, or to taste

2 scallions, white and green parts, chopped, for garnish

Chile crisp or chile oil, for garnish

Crispy Chickpeas (optional)

1 (15-ounce) can chickpeas, drained, rinsed, and patted dry

2 tablespoons extra-virgin olive oil

2 teaspoons sesame seeds

½ teaspoon each garlic powder, onion powder, and sweet paprika

½ teaspoon fine sea salt

½ teaspoon red pepper flakes

To roast the vegetables, preheat the oven to 425°F. Pile the carrots and onion on a large sheet pan. Drizzle with 1½ tablespoons of the oil, season with salt and pepper, and toss to coat evenly. Spread the vegetables in a single layer. Roast, tossing the vegetables midway through cooking, until very tender when pierced with a fork, 30 to 40 minutes.

To make the crispy chickpeas, while the carrots and onion are roasting, heat a frying pan over medium heat. When the pan is hot, add the chickpeas, olive oil, sesame seeds, garlic powder, onion powder, paprika, salt, and red pepper flakes to the pan and cook, stirring often, until the chickpeas are golden brown and crisp, about 10 minutes. Pour into a bowl and set aside. (Any leftover chickpea topping can be stored in an airtight container in the refrigerator for up to 2 days.)

To cook the aromatics, just before the carrots and onion are ready, heat a heavy, medium pot over medium-low heat and add the remaining 1½ tablespoons oil. When the oil is hot, add the garlic, ginger, and chile and cook, stirring, until fragrant, 2 to 3 minutes. Remove from the heat.

To finish the soup, add the roasted carrots and onion, broth, miso, and Golden Chedda Cashew Parm to the pot. Using an immersion blender, blend until smooth. (For a smoother soup, transfer the mixture to a high-speed blender and blend on high speed until silky smooth.) Taste and adjust the seasoning with Golden Chedda Cashew Parm, salt, and pepper if needed. Return the pot to the stovetop over medium heat, bring to a simmer, and heat until piping hot, about 5 minutes.

To serve, ladle the soup into individual bowls, top with the crispy chickpeas (if using), scallions, and chile crisp, and serve at once.

★ BREWER'S FAVORITE ★

This warm vinaigrette packs a punch with plenty of smoky bacon, briny
black olives, beer, and garlic. It'll amp up any green salad, but we particularly like it
paired with sturdy kale. The vinaigrette is also great over grilled chicken breasts.
To make the salad vegetarian, omit the bacon.

KALE SALAD
WITH OCTOBERFEST VINAIGRETTE

To cook the bacon, in a frying pan over medium heat, cook the bacon, stirring
often, until crisp, about 5 minutes. Using a slotted spoon, transfer the bacon
to paper towels to drain. Pour off all but 1 tablespoon of the fat from the pan.

To make the vinaigrette, return the pan to low heat, add the garlic, shallot,
and olives, and cook, stirring, until the garlic is golden brown, about
2 minutes. Remove the pan from the heat, add the beer, oil, and vinegar,
and stir to mix. Keep warm.

To prepare the kale, strip the kale leaves from the stalks; reserve the stalks
for another use or discard. Chop the kale leaves and transfer to a large bowl.
Season the kale with salt and, using your hands, massage the leaves to soften
them.

To assemble the salad, scatter the cranberries and reserved bacon over the
kale. Drizzle with some of the warm vinaigrette, then toss to coat evenly. Top
with the goat cheese and serve at once, passing any additional vinaigrette
alongside.

OctoberFest Vinaigrette

2 thick-cut bacon slices,
finely chopped

1 garlic clove, minced

1 small shallot, finely chopped

1 tablespoon finely chopped
dry-cured black olives

¼ cup Samuel Adams
OctoberFest or Boston Lager

¼ cup extra-virgin olive oil

2 tablespoons balsamic vinegar

Kale Salad

1 (6-ounce) bunch lacinato
(dinosaur) kale

Fine sea salt

¼ cup dried cranberries

¼ cup crumbled fresh
goat cheese

Taste the difference the addition of Everythang Sauce, an agave-based, sweet-spicy-savory flavor enhancer, makes to this classic chili recipe. **India Russell,** who shared this recipe, founded her **Everythang Sauce** company in 2019 in Springfield, Massachusetts, and the sauce soon became a favorite with foodies. If you can't get your hands on it, you can substitute a good-quality ketchup-like chili sauce. For a vegan twist with all the heartiness of a traditional chili, use vegetable broth and swap out the ground beef for a faux ground meat like Impossible Burger or Beyond Burger. The chili is great on its own or can be served over rice or with Classic Cornbread (page 171) or crackers.

BEEF CHILI WITH BEANS

To brown the onions and beef, in a large soup pot over medium-high heat, warm the oil for 2 minutes. Add the onion and cook, stirring occasionally, until translucent, about 5 minutes. Add the beef and cook, stirring occasionally and breaking up the meat into small pieces with a wooden spoon, until browned, 6 to 7 minutes.

To make the chili, add the chili powder, cumin, sugar, tomato paste, garlic powder, salt, black pepper, and cayenne pepper (if using) and stir to mix well. Add the broth, diced tomatoes with their juices, beans, and tomato sauce, stir to mix, and bring to a low boil. Reduce the heat to low and simmer gently uncovered, stirring occasionally, until slightly thickened and the flavors come together, 20 to 25 minutes.

Add the Everythang Sauce and continue to simmer, stirring often, until warmed through, about 5 minutes. Taste and adjust the seasoning with more Everythang Sauce, salt, and black pepper if needed. Remove the chili from the heat and let rest for 5 to 10 minutes.

To serve, if serving with rice, spoon rice into shallow bowls and ladle the chili over the top. Or serve the chili in bowls with cornbread or crackers alongside. Garnish with cheese and chopped red onions, if you like.

1 tablespoon olive oil

1 yellow onion, finely chopped

1 pound lean ground beef (90 percent lean)

2½ tablespoons chili powder

2 tablespoons ground cumin

2 tablespoons sugar

2 tablespoons tomato paste

1 tablespoon garlic powder

1½ teaspoons fine sea salt

½ teaspoon freshly ground black pepper

¼ teaspoon cayenne pepper (optional)

1½ cups beef broth

1 (15-ounce) can petite diced tomatoes, with juices

1 (15½-ounce) can red kidney beans, drained and rinsed

1 (8-ounce) can tomato sauce

½ cup Everythang Sauce or ketchup-like chili sauce, or more to taste

Cooked rice, cornbread, or crackers, for serving

Shredded cheddar cheese and chopped red onion or scallions, for garnish (optional)

★ BREWER'S FAVORITE ★

This version of the beloved Reuben sandwich from Boston-based chef **Ken Oringer** starts with pastrami gently warmed in Samuel Adams beer. Braised sauerkraut is amped up with onion, apple, thyme, and more beer. And in an updated twist, the toasted rye sandwich is slathered with a zesty chipotle mayonnaise and topped with melty farmhouse Cheddar. The result is an inspired fusion of traditional deli meets craft-beer innovation.

FARMHOUSE REUBEN

Braised Sauerkraut

2 tablespoons olive oil

1 yellow onion, thinly sliced

1 (12-ounce) bottle Samuel Adams OctoberFest, Boston Lager, or other marzen-style beer

1 tart-sweet baking apple, such as Granny Smith, peeled, cored, and grated

1 (16-ounce) container sauerkraut, drained and rinsed

2 fresh thyme sprigs

1 garlic clove, minced

Fine sea salt and freshly ground pepper

Sandwich Filling

½ cup Samuel Adams OctoberFest, Boston Lager, or other marzen-style beer

1 pound thinly sliced deli pastrami

½ cup mayonnaise

1 tablespoon pureed chipotle chile in adobo sauce

8 slices rye bread, lightly toasted

8 slices farmhouse Cheddar or Swiss cheese, cut to the size of the bread

To make the sauerkraut, in a frying pan over medium-low heat, warm the oil. Add the onion and cook, stirring occasionally, until lightly caramelized, about 10 minutes. Add the beer, apple, sauerkraut, thyme, and garlic, season with salt and pepper, and cook, stirring occasionally, until soft and fragrant, about 30 minutes. Remove from the heat and cover to keep warm.

Preheat the oven to 350°F.

To warm the pastrami, in a frying pan with a lid over low heat, warm the beer. Add the pastrami, cover, and let warm slowly while you ready the other ingredients.

To assemble the sandwiches, in a small bowl, stir together the mayonnaise and chipotle puree. Arrange the bread slices in a single layer on a large sheet pan and top each slice with a cheese slice. Place in the oven until the cheese melts, about 3 minutes. Remove from the oven and spread each bread slice with 1 tablespoon of the chipotle mayonnaise.

Drain the sauerkraut and the pastrami. Top 4 of the bread slices with the sauerkraut and pastrami, dividing them evenly. Cover with the remaining bread slices, cheese-mayonnaise side down, and serve at once.

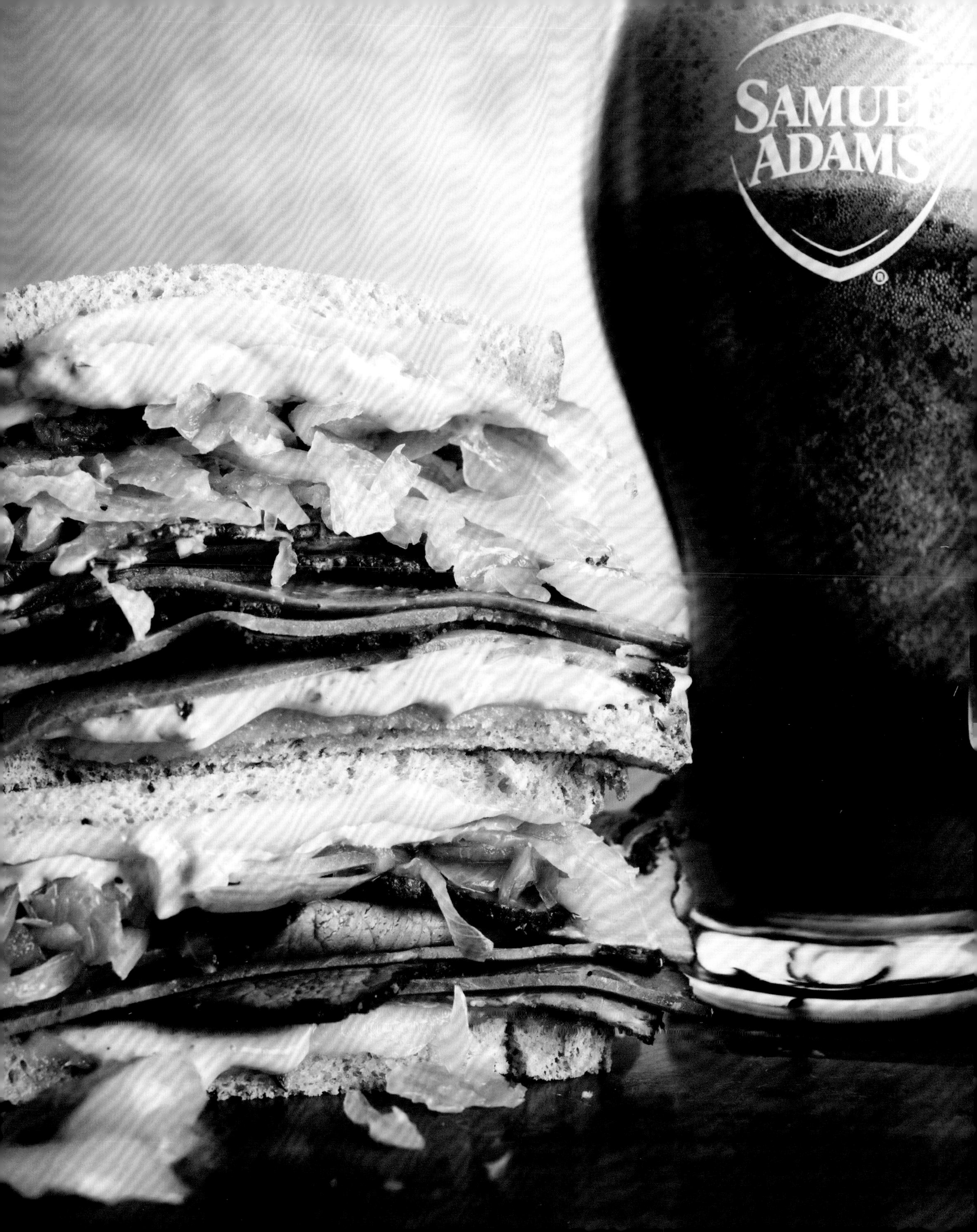
SAMUEL
ADAMS

It is often the simple things that give the most satisfaction. This updated grilled cheese sandwich makes a comforting lunch or can be cut into smaller pieces as a fun appetizer. A good-quality sourdough bread and smoky, creamy Gouda cheese are the perfect complement to the tangy hibiscus chutney, according to founder **Najeeb Muhaimin,** whose company, **Pride Road,** located in southeastern Georgia, makes the popular chutney. The family-run company uses locally sourced flowers to manufacture its line of hibiscus-based beverages, jellies, and chutneys. If you can't get their chutney, you can use another good-quality, store-bought peach chutney or other tangy chutney.

GRILLED CHEESE WITH SMOKED GOUDA & HIBISCUS CHUTNEY

8 slices sourdough bread

8 slices smoked Gouda cheese

½ cup Pride Road Original Hibiscus Chutney or Hibiscus Peach Chutney

8 tablespoons salted butter, at room temperature

To assemble the sandwiches, lay the 8 bread slices in a single layer on a work surface. Top 4 bread slices with 2 cheese slices each, covering each bread slice completely. Spread the chutney on the remaining 4 bread slices, dividing it evenly and covering each slice completely. Top each cheese-topped bread slice with a chutney bread slice, chutney side down. Spread the top of each sandwich with 1 tablespoon of the butter.

To cook the sandwiches, in a large frying pan over medium heat, melt 2 tablespoons of the butter until foaming. Add 2 sandwiches, unbuttered side down, to the pan and cook until the bottoms are golden brown, about 4 minutes. Flip the sandwiches and cook until golden brown on the second side and the filling is warmed through, about 4 minutes longer. Transfer each sandwich to a plate and serve.

Melt the remaining 2 tablespoons butter in the pan over medium heat and cook the remaining 2 sandwiches the same way. Alternatively, use 2 large frying pans and cook and serve all 4 sandwiches at the same time.

SYNOVIA JONES, FOUNDER OF NOBE'S P.B. FOODS

Synovia Jones, known affectionately as Nobe since childhood, epitomizes a lifestyle centered on health and vitality. Today, she is the driving force behind the Los Angeles–based Nobe's P.B. Foods, but her journey into plant-based cooking and veganism spans more than forty years. With a background in competitive bodybuilding and fitness instruction, Synovia has long integrated her passion for healthy living with her culinary pursuits.

Her transition to veganism was fueled by a desire to promote wellness and help others improve their diet. In 2015, she launched her first business, Super Salads to Go, offering a delectable array of fresh, organic gourmet salads. Synovia's dedication to delivering both flavor and nutrition quickly garnered attention in her community.

Inspired by the success of her salads, she expanded her menu to include enticing plant-based hot-food options, such as Vegan Crab Cake Burger and Black Bean Mushroom Burger. The rave reviews for her crab cakes caught the attention of local stores, leading to the rebranding of her business as Nobe's P.B. Foods.

Today, her vegan products are stocked by three stores, a testament to their popularity and quality. In November 2023, Synovia received a small grant to launch a mobile farmers' market, the goal of which was to address food deserts and provide fresh produce to underserved communities. The grant did not stretch to the cost of a vehicle, so she improvised by sourcing produce from local farmers and setting up a tent, leveraging her extensive experience in farmers' markets.

"I STARTED LATER IN LIFE THAN MOST IN THE CULINARY WORLD, BUT I ABSOLUTELY LOVE IT. THERE IS ALWAYS SOMETHING NEW TO LEARN AND CREATIVE WAYS TO EXPRESS. I WILL CONTINUE MY QUEST TO LEARN MORE AND SHARE MY KNOWLEDGE."

Synovia Jones

Brewing the American Dream has profoundly impacted Synovia, offering her a renewed sense of purpose and the belief that she can achieve anything. Winning the Brewing the American Dream competition opened her eyes to new possibilities and to understanding that setbacks are opportunities for growth.

Today, Nobe's P.B. Foods is on a mission to provide locally sourced, sustainable food options that are reliably delicious, nutritious, and accessible to all, especially those communities that lack easily available resources.

Chicago native **Synovia "Nobe" Jones** enjoyed many classic Sloppy Joes growing up. When she started **Nobe's P.B. Foods**, her vegan-based food business, it seemed natural to transform this traditional meat-based recipe into an entirely plant-based one. This vegan version of the cherished comfort food combines lentils, bell peppers, mushrooms, and plenty of garlic and has all the big flavors of its carnivore-friendly counterpart. The "sloppy" mix can be served atop burger buns, as it is here, or over baked potatoes or a pile of tortilla chips (don't forget the vegan cheese!).

VEGAN SLOPPY JOES

1 cup water

1 cup vegetable broth

1 cup red or green lentils

Fine sea salt and freshly ground pepper

2 tablespoons olive oil

2 small yellow onions, finely chopped

2 red bell peppers, seeded and finely chopped

2 cups finely chopped shiitake or cremini mushrooms

6 garlic cloves, minced

2 (15-ounce) cans tomato sauce

2 tablespoons coconut sugar or pure maple syrup

2 tablespoons vegan Worcestershire sauce

2 teaspoons chili powder

2 teaspoons finely chopped fresh oregano or 1 teaspoon dried oregano

1 teaspoon ground cumin

1 teaspoon garam masala (optional)

2 teaspoons smoked paprika

8 vegan burger buns, split and toasted

2 ripe but firm avocados, halved, pitted, peeled, and thinly sliced

To simmer the lentils, in a saucepan, combine the water, broth, lentils, and 1 teaspoon salt and bring to a boil over high heat. Reduce the heat to medium and simmer, stirring occasionally, until the lentils are tender but not mushy, about 15 minutes. Remove from the heat and set aside.

To cook the vegetables, while the lentils are cooking, in a large frying pan over medium heat, warm the oil. Add the onions and cook, stirring, until lightly golden, about 5 minutes. Add the bell peppers, mushrooms, and garlic, season with salt and pepper, and cook, stirring, until all the vegetables are tender, about 8 minutes.

To make the sloppy joe filling, add the tomato sauce, sugar, Worcestershire sauce, chili powder, oregano, cumin, garam masala (if using), and paprika, stir to combine, and bring to a simmer. Reduce the heat to low and simmer gently until the flavors come together, about 10 minutes.

Add the lentils and their cooking liquid to the frying pan, stir to combine, and simmer until warmed through. At this point, the lentil mixture can be cooled to room temperature and stored in an airtight container in the refrigerator for up to 4 days or in the freezer for up to 1 month and then reheated just before serving.

To assemble and serve, arrange the bun bottoms, cut side up, on individual plates. Spoon the lentil mixture onto the bun bottoms, dividing it evenly. Top with the avocado slices and close with the bun tops. Serve at once.

BREWING THE
AMERICAN DREAM
Winner

Adding cheese curds to a burger was a total revelation. This brainchild, from **Kurt Beecher Dammeier** of **Beecher's Handmade Cheese** in Washington State, pairs ground beef and pork with plenty of curds. When the meat patties are grilled, the curds soften and caramelize to perfection. The burgers are then bathed in a flavorful Boston Lager–infused chili sauce, which is equally delicious on grilled pork or chicken.

CHEESE CURD BURGERS WITH CHILI SAUCE

Boston Lager Chili Sauce

1½ teaspoons canola oil

1 large yellow onion, chopped

2 serrano chiles, chopped

6 garlic cloves, minced

1 Lapsang souchong tea bag or 2 teaspoons loose leaf tea

1½ cups pineapple juice

¾ cup Samuel Adams Boston Lager

1 (14-ounce) can crushed tomatoes, with juices

½ cup apple cider vinegar

⅓ cup dark molasses

1½ teaspoons chipotle chile powder

1½ teaspoons red pepper flakes

1½ teaspoons kosher salt

Burgers

1 pound *each* ground beef chuck and ground pork

8 ounces Beecher's cheese curds or other cheese curds, chopped

¼ cup chopped fresh parsley

Kosher salt and freshly ground black pepper

1 red onion, cut into ¼-inch-thick rings

1 teaspoon canola oil

6 burger buns, split

To make the chili sauce, in a large saucepan over medium-high heat, warm the oil. Add the onion and serrano chiles and cook, stirring, until softened and browned, about 10 minutes. Add the garlic and cook, stirring, until fragrant, about 2 minutes. If using a tea bag, slit the bag and add the tea leaves to the onion mixture. If using loose tea, measure and add to pan.

To finish the chili sauce, add the pineapple juice, beer, tomatoes with their juices, vinegar, molasses, chipotle chile powder, pepper flakes, and salt, stir well, and bring to a boil. Reduce the heat to medium-low and simmer uncovered, stirring occasionally, until the mixture is reduced by half, about 50 minutes. Remove from the heat and, using an immersion blender, puree the mixture until smooth, then cover to keep warm. The sauce can be made up to 2 weeks in advance, cooled, and stored in an airtight container in the refrigerator. Reheat before serving.

Prepare a gas or charcoal grill for direct cooking over medium-high heat (400°F to 500°F).

To make the burgers, in a large bowl, combine the beef, pork, cheese curds, parsley, 2 teaspoons salt, and ½ teaspoon black pepper. Mix gently until all the ingredients are evenly distributed. Divide into 6 equal portions and shape each portion into a patty about ¾ inch thick. Using your thumb or the back of a spoon, make a shallow indentation about 1 inch wide in the center of each patty.

To prep the onions, in a bowl, toss the onion rings with the oil, then season with salt and pepper.

To grill the onions and burgers, when the grill is ready, brush the grill grates clean. Add the onion rings to the grill over direct heat and cook, turning once or twice, until slightly charred, about 6 minutes. Transfer to a plate. Add the patties to the grill over direct heat, close the lid, and cook, turning once, until cooked to your liking, 8 to 10 minutes for medium. Transfer to the plate with the onions. Place the bun halves, cut side down, over direct heat and toast just until light golden brown. Transfer the buns, cut side up, to six plates.

To assemble the burgers, place a patty on each bun bottom. Top with warm sauce and grilled onions. Close with the buns tops and serve at once. Pass the remaining sauce on the side.

Makes 4 burgers

★ BREWER'S FAVORITE ★

For barbecue fans, every day is a good day to grill, and what's better than a juicy burger and a cold beer? In this recipe, smoky bacon, onion, and Samuel Adams Boston Lager are added to the ground beef to produce a succulent gourmet burger. Top with Cheddar and barbecue sauce or with any of your favorite burger toppings.

BACON BURGERS WITH BOSTON LAGER

Soak 2 large handfuls of apple wood chips in beer or water to cover for 30 minutes to 1 hour. Prepare a gas or charcoal grill for direct cooking over medium-high heat (400°F to 500°F).

To cook the bacon, in a frying pan over medium heat, cook the bacon, stirring occasionally, until crisp, about 6 minutes. Using a slotted spoon, transfer to paper towels to drain and cool.

To make the patties, in a large bowl, combine the beef, cooled bacon, onion, beer, salt, and pepper. Mix gently until all the ingredients are evenly distributed. Divide into 4 equal portions and shape each portion into a patty about ¾ inch thick. Using your thumb or the back of a spoon, make a shallow indentation about 1 inch wide in the center of each patty.

To grill the burgers, when the grill is ready, brush the grates clean. Add the drained wood chips directly to the coals of a charcoal grill or to the smoker box of a gas grill and close the grill lid. When smoke appears, add the patties to the grill over direct heat, close the grill lid, and cook, turning once, until cooked to your liking, 8 to 10 minutes for medium. During the last minute of grilling time, top each burger with a cheese slice. Transfer the burgers to a plate. Place the bun halves, cut side down, over direct heat and toast just until light golden brown. Transfer the buns, cut side up, to four plates.

Add condiments and toppings to the bun halves as desired and place a burger on each bun bottom. Close with the bun tops and serve at once.

8 thick-cut bacon slices, finely chopped

2 pounds lean ground beef chuck (80 percent lean)

½ cup finely chopped white onion

½ cup Samuel Adams Boston Lager

1 tablespoon fine sea salt

1 tablespoon freshly ground black pepper

4 large slices Cheddar cheese

4 hamburger buns, split

Condiments and toppings of choice for serving, such as ketchup, mustard, barbecue sauce, lettuce, tomato, red onion slices, and/or pickles

There are five basic tastes: sweet, sour, salty, bitter, and umami, which means "essence of deliciousness" in Japanese. This recipe, from Japan-born **Atsushi Nakagawa**, founder of the **Amazake Co.** in Los Angeles, uses his company's umami-rich tamari koji and shio koji seasonings to transform what might otherwise be a run-of-the-mill turkey burger into a mouthwatering treat. Atsushi is a passionate promoter of traditional Japanese foods who originally came to the United States with dreams of becoming a rock star. Quench your thirst with a chilled Samuel Adams beer while you graciously accept compliments for your culinary prowess.

UMAMI TURKEY BURGERS
WITH MUSHROOMS & ONIONS

Prepare a gas or charcoal grill for direct cooking over medium-high heat (400°F to 500°F).

To make the mushrooms, in a frying pan over medium heat, warm the oil. Add the onions and cook, stirring occasionally, until softened, about 5 minutes. Add the mushrooms and cook, stirring, until they release their liquid and are tender, about 5 minutes. Season with salt and pepper. Set aside.

To season the turkey, in a large bowl, combine the ground turkey with the 4 teaspoons shio koji. Season with a little pepper, and then mix gently to combine the ingredients. Divide into 8 equal portions and shape each portion into a patty about ¾ inch thick.

To cook the burgers, when the grill is ready, brush the grill grates clean. Add the patties to the grill over direct heat, close the grill lid, and cook, turning once, until cooked through, 8 to 10 minutes. Transfer to a plate. Place the bun halves, cut side down, over direct heat and toast just until light golden brown. Transfer the buns, cut side up, to a plate.

To assemble the burgers, in a bowl, very lightly stir together the tamari koji and mayonnaise, just until swirled together but not completely mixed. Spread the cut sides of each bun with the mayonnaise mixture, dividing it evenly. Top each bun bottom with a burger, spoon the mushroom-onion mixture on top, dividing it evenly, and finish with a small handful of arugula. Close with the bun tops and serve at once.

Note: To make a substitute for tamari koji, in a small bowl, stir together 1 tablespoon white miso and 2 tablespoons tamari or soy sauce.

1 tablespoon olive oil

2 medium yellow onions, thinly sliced

8 ounces cremini mushrooms, stem ends trimmed, then thinly sliced

Fine sea salt and freshly ground black pepper

2 pounds ground turkey

4 teaspoons Amazake Co. shio koji or ½ teaspoon fine sea salt

8 burger buns, split

6 teaspoons Amazake Co. tamari koji (see Note)

½ cup mayonnaise or aioli, for spreading

2 cups baby arugula

★ BREWER'S FAVORITE ★

Bratwurst, a German-style pork "frying sausage," is the star of this generously laden sandwich. The sausage is simmered in a bath of Samuel Adams beer and sliced onion, then tucked into a toasted roll and topped with a tangle of quickly cooked onions and bell peppers to produce a sandwich that is ideal for any laid-back gathering or game night. Add any condiments and toppings you like. One good option is the Braised Sauerkraut for the Farmhouse Reuben on page 86.

BRAT SANDWICHES WITH PEPPERS & ONIONS

3 cups (24 ounces) Samuel Adams OctoberFest or Boston Lager

2 large white or yellow onions, halved and sliced

8 fresh bratwursts

2 tablespoons canola oil

2 red bell peppers, seeded, quartered, and sliced

Fine sea salt and freshly ground pepper

8 torpedo rolls, split and lightly toasted

Country Dijon or grainy mustard, for spreading

To simmer the bratwursts, in a large saucepan over medium-high heat, combine the beer, half of the onions, and the bratwursts and bring just to a boil. Reduce the heat to low and simmer gently until the brats are cooked through and hot, 10 to 15 minutes.

To cook the onions and bell peppers, in a frying pan over medium heat, heat the oil. Add the remaining onion and the bell peppers, season with salt and pepper, and cook, stirring occasionally, until tender, about 10 minutes.

To assemble the sandwiches, spread the cut sides of each roll with mustard. Using a slotted spoon or tongs, lift the brats from the poaching liquid and nestle them in the rolls. Top with the pepper-onion mixture, dividing it evenly, and serve right away.

Not your average lobster roll, this recipe elevates the luxurious sweetness of fresh lobster with a unique twist: a sprinkle of lemon salt. The salt blend not only enhances the flavor of the seafood but also adds zesty brightness, setting it apart from traditional recipes. Both the recipe and the salt come from **Anna Eves,** founder of **Cape Ann Sea Salt Co.** All of Anna's salts are hand harvested and solar evaporated on Cape Ann in Rockport, Massachusetts. If you can't find her lemon salt, you can make your own (see Note).

LOBSTER ROLLS WITH LEMON SALT

To prepare the lobster filling, cut the lobster meat into bite-size pieces, then transfer to a bowl. Add the mayonnaise, pepper, and lemon salt and stir gently to coat the lobster evenly. Cover and refrigerate for at least 30 minutes or up to 2 hours.

To toast the buns, spread the butter on the cut side of the hot dog buns, dividing it evenly. Warm a griddle or large frying pan over medium heat. Add the buns to the griddle and toast, turning once, until the sides are nicely browned. Transfer the buns, split-top side side up, to a wire rack so they don't get soggy.

To assemble the rolls, remove the lobster from the refrigerator and divide evenly among the buns. Sprinkle a little more lemon salt on top, then serve right away.

Note: To prepare your own lemon salt, in a bowl, combine 2 tablespoons fine sea salt with 1 teaspoon finely grated lemon zest. Work the zest into the salt with the back of a spoon until the salt turns a nice lemon chiffon color. Transfer to a small jar, cap tightly, and store in a cool, dry place for up to 6 months.

1 pound cooked fresh lobster meat

2 tablespoons mayonnaise

¼ teaspoon freshly ground black pepper

¼ teaspoon Cape Ann Sea Salt Co. lemon salt, plus more for serving

2 tablespoons salted butter, at room temperature

4 split-top hot dog buns

ENTERPRISING **ENTREES**

Makes 6 servings

★ BREWER'S FAVORITE ★

Traditionally British, and originally served generously sprinkled with salt, doused with malt vinegar, and wrapped in newspaper at the local "chip shop," this is a dish we never tire of. We recommend using cod or haddock, but halibut or hake also works. Samuel Adams Boston Lager or Golden Pilsner beer goes into the batter both for its flavor and for its carbonation and maltiness, which produces a lighter, crispier, and tastier coating. Enjoy with deliciously thick deep-fried potatoes and plenty of cold beer.

FISH & CHIPS

To prepare the potatoes, peel the potatoes and cut lengthwise into ½-inch-thick planks. Cut each plank lengthwise into ½-inch-wide strips. In a large bowl, combine the potatoes with cold water to cover and let sit for 10 minutes. Drain the potatoes and pat dry with paper towels.

To par-fry the chips, line a large sheet pan with paper towels. Into a large, heavy saucepan, pour oil to a depth of at least 2 inches (but do not fill more than half full) and heat over medium-high heat to 250°F on a deep-frying thermometer. Working in batches to avoid crowding, fry the potatoes, turning once or twice, until very lightly golden, about 5 minutes. Using a slotted spoon or wire skimmer, transfer to the paper towel–lined pan to drain. Reserve the oil in the pan.

Preheat the oven to 200°F. Set a wire rack on a second sheet pan and place in the oven.

To fry the chips a second time, increase the heat of the oil to 325°F. Working in batches to avoid crowding, fry the potatoes again, turning once or twice, until golden brown and cooked through, about 3 minutes. Remove the rack-pan setup from the oven and transfer the chips to the rack, sprinkle immediately with salt, and return the rack-pan setup to the oven. Repeat until all the potatoes are fried and keep warm in the oven while you fry the fish. Reserve the oil in the pan.

To make the beer batter, in a wide, shallow bowl, whisk together the flour, beer, salt, and pepper until smooth and the consistency of heavy cream. Line the first sheet pan with fresh paper towels. Heat the reserved oil to 325°F.

To fry the fish, working in batches to avoid crowding, dip each piece of fish into the batter, coating completely and allowing the excess to drip off. Carefully add the battered fish to the hot oil and fry, turning once or twice, until the fish is crispy, golden brown, and cooked through, 2 to 3 minutes. Using tongs, transfer to the paper towel–lined pan to drain.

Serve the fish and chips at once with tartar sauce, lemons, and/or vinegar.

Chips

2 pounds russet potatoes, peeled

Canola or peanut oil, for deep-frying

Fine sea salt

Beer-Battered Fish

2 cups all-purpose flour

2¼ cups Samuel Adams Boston Lager, Wicked Easy, or Golden Pilsner

2 teaspoons fine sea salt

2 teaspoons freshly ground black pepper

2½ pounds fresh or thawed frozen cod or haddock fillets

Tartar sauce, lemon wedges, and/or malt vinegar, for serving

Makes 8 tacos

This updated take on steak tacos combines blackberry jam–glazed skirt steak topped with a fresh cabbage, blackberry, and pear slaw and crumbled blue cheese. The recipe comes from **Ashley Rouse,** founder of **Trade Street Jam Co.,** a woman- and Black-owned business based in Brooklyn, New York. It calls for the company's Blackberry Mulled Merlot jam, which lends a particularly fragrant flavor to the steak, but a natural or homemade blackberry jam can be substituted in a pinch. These sweet-salty tacos are guaranteed to be a Tuesday night repeat!

STEAK TACOS WITH BLACKBERRY PEAR SLAW

Slaw

¼ cup olive oil

¼ cup red wine vinegar

Juice of 1 lime

1 teaspoon sugar or honey

1½ cups shredded red cabbage

1 cup shredded green cabbage

2 cups blackberries, halved

1 Bartlett pear, peeled, cored, and cut into matchsticks

¼ red onion, thinly sliced

Tacos

1 pound skirt steak

Kosher salt and freshly cracked pepper

2 tablespoons olive oil

⅓ cup Trade Street Jam Co. Blackberry Mulled Merlot Jam or natural blackberry jam, plus more for drizzling

8 corn tortillas, about 6 inches in diameter

Flaky sea salt, for garnish

½ cup crumbled blue cheese

1 tablespoon chopped fresh chives

To make the slaw, in a small bowl, whisk together the oil, vinegar, lime juice, and sugar until the sugar dissolves. In a medium bowl, toss together the red and green cabbage, blackberries, pear, and red onion. Drizzle the dressing over the cabbage mixture and toss to coat well. Set aside.

To sear the steak, heat a large cast-iron frying pan over medium-high heat. Season the steak all over with kosher salt and pepper. When the pan is hot, add the oil. When the oil is shimmering, add the steak and cook, turning once, until well seared on both sides and cooked to your liking, 6 to 8 minutes total for medium-rare. Transfer to a cutting board and immediately brush the top of the steak with the jam. Let rest for 10 minutes.

Warm the tortillas while the steak is resting. Heat a dry, clean frying pan over medium heat. One at a time, add the tortillas to the hot pan and heat, turning once, for 20 to 30 seconds on each side. As they are ready, stack them on a sheet of aluminum foil and wrap to keep warm.

To assemble the tacos, thinly slice the steak against the grain. To assemble the tacos, divide the slaw evenly among the warm tortillas, then top with the steak. Sprinkle the steak with flaky salt and top with the cheese and chives, dividing them evenly. Drizzle with jam (if the jam is too thick to drizzle, warm it slightly). Serve at once.

ASHLEY STEWART, OWNER OF COLONEL DE GOURMET HERBS & SPICES

Colonel De Gourmet Herbs & Spices is a family business rooted in a legacy of culinary passion and expertise. Founded by De Stewart, a Kentucky colonel with a lifelong love of food, the business began as a humble endeavor at farmers' markets in 2005. De's vision was fueled by his experiences working in his family's markets and by his desire to showcase the transformative power of herbs and spices in everyday cooking.

With a flair for entrepreneurship, De decided to pitch a cooking show highlighting the flavorsome potential of spices and herbs to a local cable channel. The show was a success and sparked interest in his products, prompting the launch of Colonel De Gourmet Herbs & Spices in 2006 at the historic Findlay Market in Cincinnati.

Over the years, the business flourished, expanding its offerings to over five hundred meticulously curated products, from spices to salts, meat rubs to teas, sauces to marinades. De's dedication to quality and innovation earned him a place in the hearts of the northern Kentucky and Cincinnati culinary community. His passing in 2018 left a void, but his legacy lives on through his family's ongoing commitment to his vision.

Today, Colonel De Gourmet Herbs & Spices continues to thrive under the leadership of De's wife, known affectionately as Mrs. Colonel, and their son, Ashley. Their dedication to preserving De's legacy is evident in their

> "BEING INVOLVED WITH BREWING THE AMERICAN DREAM HAS HELPED OUR BUSINESS GROW. THE SPEED COACHING SESSIONS, ESPECIALLY WITH EXPERTS FROM SAMUEL ADAMS, HAVE BEEN A STANDOUT EVERY YEAR. THESE SESSIONS OFFER GREAT ADVICE, LEAVING US PUMPED TO TRY OUT FRESH IDEAS. THE KNOWLEDGE AND EXCITEMENT WE'VE GAINED HAVE BEEN KEY TO OUR SUCCESS."

Ashley Stewart

commitment to offering high-quality products and exceptional service to customers.

As a proud participant in the Brewing the American Dream program, Colonel De Gourmet Herbs & Spices is grateful for the invaluable support and mentorship it has received. The knowledge gained has empowered everyone at the company to continue serving the community with passion and excellence and to carry forward their founder's legacy.

With flavors of allspice, garlic, coriander, and lemon—reminiscent of Jamaican jerk seasoning—**Colonel De's** Samuel Adams OctoberFest Rub is a natural on roasted or grilled chicken. What makes this particular blend even more special is its origin: it was discovered in an old recipe binder filled with unique creations by none other than Colonel De himself! Whether you're hosting a family dinner, a backyard barbecue, or a game-day feast, this recipe for a whole chicken roasted atop a can of beer from owner **Ashley Stewart** is sure to impress. Depending on the time of year, you can make this with the OctoberFest Rub (in the fall) or use Colonel De's Summer Ale Rub (in the summer). Be sure to use a can of the corresponding beer to match the rub!

BEER CAN CHICKEN

1 whole chicken, about 4 pounds

3 tablespoons olive oil

4 tablespoons Colonel De's Samuel Adams OctoberFest Rub or Summer Ale Rub or other smoky barbecue chicken rub

1 (12-ounce) can Samuel Adams OctoberFest, Summer Ale, or Boston Lager

To prep the chicken, position a rack in the lower third of the oven and preheat the oven to 350°F. Pat the chicken dry with paper towels. Brush the chicken all over with the oil, then rub with 3 tablespoons of the rub, coating the bird completely.

Pour out (or drink!) ½ cup of the beer from the can. Add the remaining 1 tablespoon rub to the can of beer and swirl to mix.

To roast the chicken, slide the chicken, legs down, over the open can and place the can in a small roasting pan or a cast-iron frying pan. Roast the chicken until golden brown and the juices run clear when a thigh is pierced near the bone, 1¼ to 1½ hours. (An instant-read thermometer inserted into the thickest part of the thigh—not touching bone—should register 165°F.)

When the chicken is ready, remove the pan from the oven and let the chicken rest on the beer can in the pan for 10 minutes. Lift the chicken off the can and transfer to a cutting board. Carve and serve.

Simple yet elegant, this dish seasons chicken thighs with fragrant garlic truffle salt, then roasts them alongside fingerling potatoes with fresh rosemary in a lemon-caper sauce. This one-pan meal for a cozy dinner is shared by **Sydney Karp Poll,** founder of Chicago-based **SydPlayEat,** which offers a range of black truffle hot sauces and seasoning salts to help home cooks add new flavors to their menus.

CHICKEN THIGHS & POTATOES
WITH GARLIC TRUFFLE SALT

4 large bone-in, skin-on chicken thighs (each about 6 ounces)

1 teaspoon SydSalt Garlic Breath Garlic Truffle Salt, plus more as needed (see Note)

⅓ cup plus 3 tablespoons avocado oil

¼ cup fresh lemon juice

1 tablespoon finely chopped garlic

1½ teaspoons capers

1 pound small fingerling or golden potatoes

3 fresh rosemary sprigs

Crusty bread, for serving (optional)

Preheat the oven to 450°F.

Season the chicken thighs all over with the garlic truffle salt. In a bowl, whisk together ⅓ cup of the oil, lemon juice, garlic, and capers.

To sear the chicken and potatoes, in a large cast-iron frying pan over medium-high heat, warm the remaining 3 tablespoons oil. When the oil is hot, add the chicken, skin side down, along with the potatoes and rosemary sprigs. Cook the chicken until the skin side is golden brown, about 10 minutes. Flip the chicken skin side up and stir the potatoes. Pour the oil–lemon juice mixture over the chicken and potatoes.

To finish the chicken and potatoes, transfer the pan to the oven and roast until the chicken is cooked through and the potatoes are tender, about 40 minutes. (An instant-read thermometer inserted into the thickest part of a thigh—not touching bone—should register 165°F.)

Bring the pan to the table and let your guests serve themselves, sprinkling with more garlic truffle salt if desired. Accompany with bread, if desired, for dipping into the delicious lemon-caper-garlic sauce.

Note: If you don't have garlic truffle salt, use 1 teaspoon mixed garlic powder, fine sea salt, and freshly ground black pepper.

A great choice for a backyard barbecue, your next tailgate, or a neighborhood potluck, this flavor-packed grilled chicken gets its zesty character from a good dose of Hillside Harvest Sun Kissed Tomato Hot Sauce. Created by **Hillside Harvest** founder **Kamaal Jarrett,** the smooth and savory sauce, a balanced mix of chiles, sun-dried tomatoes, olive oil, vinegar, and sea salt, bears many of the hallmarks of the Caribbean cuisine of his Jamaican homeland.

BBQ CHICKEN WITH SUN-KISSED SAUCE

To season the chicken, place the legs on a large sheet pan and pat dry with paper towels. Season the chicken all over with salt. Let the chicken rest at room temperature while you light the grill and make the barbecue sauce.

Prepare a gas or charcoal grill for direct and indirect cooking over medium-high heat (400°F to 450°F).

To make the sauce, in a small saucepan over medium heat, melt the butter. Add the garlic and cook, stirring constantly, until the garlic is sizzling and fragrant, about 30 seconds. Add the tomato paste and cook, stirring constantly and scraping the bottom of the pan to prevent scorching, until the paste caramelizes to a darker rust red, 1 to 2 minutes. Add the hot sauce, maple syrup, soy sauce, Worcestershire sauce, vinegar, and a pinch of salt, stir well, and bring to a boil. Reduce the heat to medium-low and simmer gently, stirring occasionally, for 5 minutes.

Remove the sauce from the heat. Spoon or pour half of the sauce into a small heatproof ramekin and set aside. Reserve the remaining sauce for basting the chicken on the grill.

To grill the chicken, when the grill is ready, brush the grill grates clean. Add the chicken to the grill over direct heat, close the grill lid, and cook, turning about every 2 minutes, until the chicken is browned on both sides, about 10 minutes. Move the chicken, skin side up, to indirect heat. Continue grilling the chicken, with the lid closed, until the chicken is cooked through, about 25 minutes total. (An instant-read thermometer inserted into the thickest part of a thigh—not touching bone—should register 165°F.)

To baste the chicken, about 15 minutes before it is ready, use a grilling brush to evenly baste the chicken with the reserved sauce. Continue basting and turning the chicken every 5 minutes over indirect heat, with the lid closed, until the barbecue sauce is sticky and caramelized. Discard any remaining sauce used for basting.

To serve, transfer the grilled chicken to a platter and serve with the reserved ramekin of sauce.

4 whole chicken legs (thigh and drumstick), about 12 ounces each

Fine sea salt

2 tablespoons unsalted butter

3 garlic cloves, minced

¼ cup tomato paste

¼ cup Hillside Harvest Sun Kissed Tomato hot sauce or a mild hot sauce of your choice

¼ cup pure maple syrup

2 tablespoons soy sauce

2 tablespoons Worcestershire sauce

2 tablespoons apple cider vinegar

Makes 4 to 6 servings

A vibrant Tex-Mex dish, migas is a heady mix of crispy tortilla strips, spicy chorizo, and soft scrambled eggs with a pop of colorful pico de gallo. New England–based **Amanda Bauman,** the founder of **Chica de Gallo,** brings this festive recipe to life, offering a flavorful start to your day that looks as inviting as it is delicious. To make the dish vegan, substitute plant-based chorizo, liquid plant-based eggs, and vegan cheese. In a pinch, broken, store-bought tortilla chips can be used in place of the fresh-fried tortillas—skip the first step of the recipe and use only 1 tablespoon oil to cook the chorizo.

MIGAS WITH CHORIZO

To fry the tortilla strips, line a plate with paper towels and set it near the stove. In a frying pan over medium heat, warm the oil. Add the tortilla strips and cook, turning as needed, until crispy, about 2 minutes. Transfer to the paper towel–lined plate to drain; reserve the oil.

To brown the chorizo, with the pan still over medium heat, add the chorizo. Cook, stirring occasionally and breaking up any large chunks, until lightly browned, 6 to 8 minutes.

To cook the eggs, in a bowl, whisk together the eggs and milk. When the chorizo is ready, add the egg mixture, pico de gallo, and reserved tortilla strips and stir gently over medium heat until the eggs are cooked to your liking, about 5 minutes.

Offer as many toppings as you like in small bowls at the table for guests to add as desired. Spoon the migas onto a platter or individual plates and serve immediately.

2 tablespoons canola or avocado oil

6 corn tortillas, each about 6 inches in diameter, cut into ½-inch-wide strips

1 pound fresh chorizo, casing removed, crumbled

8 large eggs

2 tablespoons milk or water

1 (14-ounce) container Chica de Gallo pico de gallo or your favorite pico de gallo, drained

Toppings (optional)

Chica De Gallo Guacamole or your favorite guacamole

Your favorite roasted tomato or tomatillo salsa

Shredded Monterey jack or Cheddar cheese

Avocado slices

Crema or sour cream

Hot sauce

★ BREWER'S FAVORITE ★

Masterful seasoning, a slow simmer, and a savory mustard-and-onion sauce make these pork chops craveworthy. A darker Samuel Adams beer, such as OctoberFest, Winter Lager, or Chocolate Bock, is the ideal simmering medium, with the bold character of the beer amplifying the richness of the meat. Braised Red Cabbage with Beer & Apples (page 165) or Brussels Sprouts with Bacon & OctoberFest (page 170) would make an excellent side.

PORK CHOPS WITH MUSTARD & ONIONS

4 thick-cut bone-in pork rib chops (2 to 3 pounds total)

1 teaspoon dried dill

1 teaspoon yellow mustard powder

1 teaspoon fine sea salt

½ teaspoon freshly ground pepper

1 tablespoon olive oil

1 large yellow onion, thinly sliced

1½ cups Samuel Adams OctoberFest, Winter Lager, or Chocolate Bock

1 tablespoon malt or apple cider vinegar

2 tablespoons whole-grain mustard

½ cup sour cream

Chopped fresh dill, for garnish

Season the chops all over with the dried dill, mustard powder, salt, and pepper.

To brown the chops, in a large, heavy frying pan over high heat, warm the oil. When the oil is hot, add the chops and cook, turning once, until browned on both sides, 2 to 3 minutes on each side. Transfer the chops to a plate, leaving the fat in the pan.

To cook the onion, reduce the heat to medium-low and add the onion to the pan. Cover the pan and cook, stirring occasionally, until soft, about 10 minutes.

Arrange the chops on top of the onion, pour in the beer and vinegar, re-cover, reduce the heat to low, and simmer until the meat is quite tender, about 30 minutes. Transfer the chops to a platter and cover to keep warm.

To finish the sauce and serve, add the whole-grain mustard to the pan, stir well, increase the heat to medium, and cook, stirring often, until the sauce is reduced to a syrupy consistency. Remove the pan from the heat, stir in the sour cream, and pour the sauce over the chops. Garnish with fresh dill and serve right away.

SAMUEL ADAMS
OCTOBERFEST

In 1810, the people of Munich threw a party so great that they've been doing it ever since, and we've captured the timeless taste of that annual celebration long known as Oktoberfest. Rich and roasty, Samuel Adams OctoberFest is a cheer to fall and over two hundred years of fall festivities. Our take on the style blends hearty malts with light hops, creating a liquid signal to make the most of the cooler days ahead. It boasts a smooth flavor with notes of caramel, a deep amber color, and a mild, pleasant sweetness that will accompany you from August through October. It's great for the season—or for whatever you're celebrating.

MAKES 1 ALE-TAIL
OCTOBERFEST PINEAPPLE ZINGER

1 ounce tequila or mezcal
¾ ounce pineapple juice
½ ounce fresh lime juice
½ ounce cinnamon simple syrup
or plain simple syrup
3 ounces Samuel Adams OctoberFest
1 cinnamon stick

In a cocktail shaker, combine the tequila, pineapple juice, lime juice, and cinnamon simple-syrup. Fill the shaker with ice and shake vigorously until well mixed.

Fill a highball glass with ice, then strain the tequila mixture into the glass. Top with the OctoberFest. Garnish with a flaming cinnamon stick, resting over the top of the glass, and serve immediately.

Cinnamon Simple Syrup: Combine ½ cup sugar and ½ cup water in a pot over medium heat. Whisk until sugar has dissolved. Add 1 cinnamon stick and simmer on low for 10 minutes; do not let boil. Remove from the heat and let cool with the cinnamon stick still in. Once cool, remove the cinnamon stick and store in the fridge.

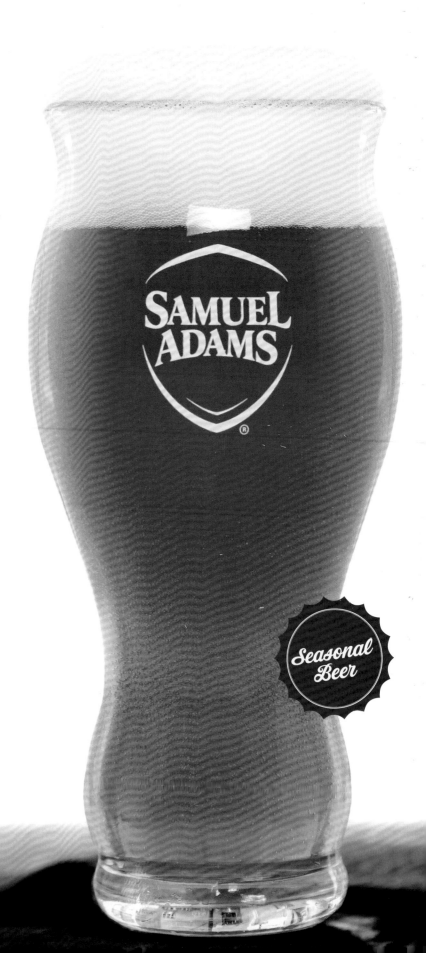

Seasonal Beer

Started by a trio of friends in 2017, Massachusetts-based **Little Trúc** makes a wonderful array of Southeast Asian–inspired fresh curry pastes and chile condiments that outshine their typical market counterparts. The green curry paste contains fresh green chiles, makrut lime leaves, lemongrass, garlic, cilantro, cardamom, coriander seeds, and more for a result that is spicy, bright, and floral. Cofounder **Katrina Pierson** suggests serving this vibrant chicken and eggplant dish over steamed jasmine rice. Feel free to add other blanched or sautéed vegetables as you like.

GREEN CURRY CHICKEN
WITH EGGPLANT & BASIL

To make the curry base, in a medium saucepan over medium heat, combine ½ cup of the coconut milk and the coconut oil and bring to a simmer. Cook until slightly thickened, about 1 minute. Stir in the curry paste and cook, stirring occasionally, until the oil begins to separate from the paste and is visible on the surface of the mixture, 5 to 6 minutes.

To assemble and simmer the curry, add the remaining 2½ cups of the coconut milk, the water, chicken, eggplant, and whole lime leaves and stir well. Season with the fish sauce and palm sugar to taste. Increase the heat to medium-high and bring to a simmer, then reduce the heat to a gentle simmer and cook until the chicken is cooked through, the eggplant is softened, and the coconut oil begins to separate, 10 to 12 minutes.

To serve, remove from the heat and stir in the basil leaves. Serve over rice and garnish with the sliced lime leaves.

3 cups coconut milk, preferably from a carton

2 tablespoons coconut oil

1 (5-ounce) pouch Little Trúc Green Curry Paste or ¼ cup Thai green curry paste

½ cup water

1 pound boneless, skinless chicken thighs, excess fat trimmed and cut into 2-inch pieces

6 small Thai eggplants, stemmed and quartered, or 1 Asian eggplant, stemmed and cut into 1-inch chunks

4 or 5 fresh makrut lime leaves, plus 2 leaves, stem and rib removed, then thinly sliced, for garnish

2 to 3 tablespoons fish sauce

1 to 2 tablespoons palm sugar or firmly packed light brown sugar

Large handful of fresh Thai basil leaves

Steamed jasmine rice, for serving

This Bolognese-inspired recipe was created by **Jennifer and Giacomo Vascotto,** founders of **Trenchers Farmhouse,** a farm-to-table maker of artisanal fresh pasta and pasta sauces in northeastern Vermont. It calls for topping their house-made fresh pasta with a hearty vodka-scented sauce of Italian sausage and grated turnips. A big, hollow pasta like rigatoni works especially well with the rich, creamy sauce. Buon appetito!

RIGATONI WITH SAUSAGE & TURNIPS

2 teaspoons avocado or vegetable oil

12 ounces sweet or spicy Italian sausages, casings removed

4 tablespoons unsalted butter

2 to 3 white turnips (about 1 pound total), unpeeled and shredded on the large holes of a box grater-shredder

1 medium yellow onion, finely chopped

3 garlic cloves, minced

Kosher salt

2 to 2½ cups water

½ cup vodka

1¼ cups heavy cream

½ teaspoon freshly grated nutmeg

1 to 2 teaspoons balsamic vinegar, plus more if needed

1 tablespoon finely chopped fresh sage

1 tablespoon finely chopped fresh flat-leaf parsley

1 tablespoon finely chopped fresh oregano

1 teaspoon freshly ground pepper, plus more for serving

14 ounces Trenchers Farmhouse fresh rigatoni or other fresh rigatoni pasta

Freshly grated Parmesan cheese, for serving

To brown the sausage, line a plate with paper towels and set it near the stove. In a large cast-iron frying pan over medium-high heat, warm the oil. Crumble the sausage into the pan and cook, stirring occasionally and breaking up the meat with a wooden spoon or spatula, until golden brown, 2 to 4 minutes. Using a slotted spoon, transfer the sausage to the paper towel–lined plate. Pour out any fat from the pan.

To make the sauce, reduce the heat to medium and add the butter to the pan. Cook, stirring, until the butter turns dark golden brown, about 3 minutes. Add the turnips, onion, garlic, and 1½ teaspoons salt, stir well, and cook, stirring, until the turnips are tender and light golden brown, about 10 minutes.

Add 2 cups of the water to the pan, reduce the heat to medium-low, and simmer gently, stirring occasionally, until the water has evaporated, 25 to 30 minutes. The turnip mixture should be soft and very tender. If it is not, add the remaining ½ cup water and continue to cook, stirring occasionally, until the mixture is dry, about 10 minutes longer.

To finish the sauce, when the turnip mixture is dry, remove the pan from the heat and add the vodka. Return the pan to medium-low heat, bring to a simmer, and cook, stirring often, until the alcohol has burned off, 2 to 3 minutes. Add 1 cup of the cream, the reserved sausage, and the nutmeg and continue to simmer, stirring occasionally, until the cream is reduced by half, about 20 minutes. Stir in the remaining ¼ cup cream and the balsamic vinegar to taste along with the sage, parsley, oregano, and pepper.

To make the rigatoni, while the sauce is cooking, bring a large pot two-thirds full of salted water to a boil over high heat. Add the rigatoni to the boiling water and cook, stirring occasionally, until al dente, according to the package directions. Scoop out and reserve ½ cup of the pasta water, then drain the pasta.

Add the pasta to the sauce along with enough of the reserved pasta water (a spoonful at a time) to loosen the sauce to the consistency you like. Simmer the sauce and pasta over medium-low heat, stirring, until the sauce coats the pasta and thickens slightly, 2 to 3 minutes. Taste and adjust the seasoning with more salt and balsamic vinegar if needed. Serve at once, topped with pepper and Parmesan cheese.

Ideal for a summer barbecue menu, these tender, juicy chicken kebabs are treated to a heady marinade of bourbon, porter, soy sauce, and mustard before they hit the grill. Adding bell pepper and red onion to the skewers contributes both color and flavor. Try the kebabs alongside Spicy Calypso Rice (page 175) or over fluffy couscous.

CHICKEN KEBABS
WITH BEER-BOURBON MARINADE

To marinate the chicken, in a bowl, whisk together the beer, bourbon, soy sauce, scallions, mustard, brown sugar, Worcestershire sauce, salt, and pepper. Add the chicken pieces and stir to coat evenly. Cover and refrigerate for at least 30 minutes or up to 4 hours.

If using bamboo skewers, soak in cold water for 30 minutes.

Prepare a gas or charcoal grill for direct cooking over medium-high heat (400°F to 450°F). Remove the chicken from the marinade. Thread the chicken pieces onto skewers, alternating them with pieces of bell pepper and red onion.

To grill the kebabs, when the grill is ready, brush the grill grates clean. Add the kebabs to the grill over direct heat, close the grill lid, and cook, turning occasionally, until nicely charred and the chicken is cooked through, about 10 minutes. Transfer to a platter and serve.

½ cup Samuel Adams Boston Lager

¼ cup bourbon

¼ cup soy sauce

¼ cup minced scallions, white and green parts

2 tablespoons Dijon or whole-grain mustard

3 tablespoons firmly packed light brown sugar

2 teaspoons Worcestershire sauce

½ teaspoon fine sea salt

½ teaspoon freshly ground pepper

2 pounds boneless, skinless chicken thighs, trimmed of excess fat and cut into 1-inch pieces

1 large red bell pepper, halved, seeded, and cut into 1½-inch pieces

½ large red onion, cut into 1½-inch pieces

Makes 6 servings

★ BREWER'S FAVORITE ★

These beef-and-pork meatballs are an ideal centerpiece for a warm, cozy meal at home. A generous splash of Samuel Adams OctoberFest adds flavor and depth to the creamy mushroom sauce, imparting a malty sweetness to every bite. Serve with mashed potatoes or buttered egg noodles.

MEATBALLS WITH MUSHROOM BEER SAUCE

Meatballs
½ cup minced yellow onion

2 tablespoons Samuel Adams OctoberFest

2 garlic cloves, minced

½ teaspoon dried thyme

½ teaspoon red pepper flakes

Kosher salt and freshly ground black pepper

1 pound each ground beef chuck and ground pork

2 large eggs, lightly beaten

⅔ cup fine dried bread crumbs

¼ cup finely chopped parsley

¼ cup olive oil, for frying

Sauce
2 tablespoons olive oil

2 yellow onions, halved and thinly sliced

8 ounces cremini mushrooms, sliced

¼ cup all-purpose flour

1⅓ cups beef broth, warmed

1 cup Samuel Adams OctoberFest

1 cup sour cream

1 tablespoon Worcestershire sauce

1 tablespoon sweet paprika

¼ cup finely chopped fresh parsley, for garnish

To make the meatballs, in a large bowl, combine the onion, beer, garlic, thyme, red pepper flakes, 1 teaspoon salt, and 1 teaspoon black pepper. Set aside for 15 minutes for the flavors to develop. Add the beef, pork, eggs, bread crumbs, and parsley to the bowl and, using your hands or a large spoon, mix well. Cover and refrigerate for at least 1 hour or up to 4 hours.

To make the sauce, in a Dutch oven or other large, heavy pot over medium heat, warm the oil. Add the onions and cook, stirring often, until golden brown and lightly caramelized, 10 to 12 minutes. Add the mushrooms and continue to cook, stirring often, just until tender, about 5 minutes. Sprinkle the flour over the onion-mushroom mixture, stir to mix, and cook, stirring constantly, until the mixture is golden brown, about 4 minutes. Slowly add the broth while stirring constantly. Continue to cook, stirring, until the mixture thickens slightly, about 2 minutes. Reduce the heat to medium-low and stir in the beer, sour cream, Worcestershire sauce, and paprika, mixing well. Do not let the sauce boil. Season with salt and pepper, remove from the heat, and cover to keep warm.

To form the meatballs, between dampened palms, roll the meat mixture into balls about 1 inch in diameter.

To fry the meatballs, heat a large, heavy frying pan over medium heat. When the pan is hot, add the olive oil and swirl the pan to coat the bottom evenly. Add as many meatballs to the pan as will fit comfortably without crowding and cook, turning as needed, until evenly browned on all sides. As the meatballs are ready, transfer them to the pot holding the sauce. Repeat until all the meatballs are browned.

To simmer the meatballs, when all the meatballs are in the sauce, place the pot over medium heat and bring the sauce just to a simmer. Reduce the heat to low, cover, and simmer gently until the meatballs are cooked through and the flavors are nicely blended, 45 to 60 minutes. Serve right away, garnished with the parsley.

Shepherd's pie—traditionally well-seasoned minced lamb or beef topped with mashed potatoes—is both one of the great British comfort foods and popular pub fare. This plant-based version from **Sandra Mathis** at **Grace Kelli Cupcakes**, based in New York City, reflects her aim to offer "old-fashioned" taste inspired by family recipes. Loaded with fresh vegetables, this hearty, satisfying dish is the ideal ace up your sleeve when you need a nutritious meal at the end of a busy day.

VEGAN SHEPHERD'S PIE

Preheat the oven to 425°F. Grease a 9 x 13-inch baking dish with vegan butter.

To make the mashed potatoes, in a large saucepan, combine the potatoes with water to cover, add 1 tablespoon salt, and bring to a boil over high heat, stirring occasionally. Reduce the heat to medium-low and boil gently until the potatoes are tender but not mushy, about 10 minutes. Drain the potatoes in a fine-mesh sieve, then return to the saucepan. Using a potato masher, roughly mash the potatoes. Add the ½ cup vegan butter and continue mashing until the butter melts. Add the milk and continue to mash until the potatoes are smooth and creamy, adding more milk if needed to achieve a creamy consistency. Season with salt and pepper and stir to combine. Cover and set aside.

To make the filling, in a frying pan over medium heat, warm the oil. Add the onion, carrots, zucchini, yellow squash, red and yellow bell peppers, and garlic, then season with salt. Cook, stirring often, until the vegetables are tender-crisp, about 5 minutes. Add the tomato sauce and thyme, stir well, and season with salt and pepper. Stir in the cornstarch mixture, mixing well, and bring the mixture to a simmer. Reduce the heat to low and cook gently, stirring occasionally, until the mixture thickens, about 4 minutes. Add the Worcestershire sauce and vinegar and continue to cook, stirring, for 3 minutes longer. Remove from the heat and transfer to the prepared baking dish, spreading the filling in an even layer.

Transfer the mashed potatoes to a large piping bag fitted with a large star tip. Pipe the potatoes over the vegetable filling, covering it completely. Alternatively, spoon the potatoes over the filling, then gently spread into an even layer, creating texture with the tines of a fork.

Bake until the filling is bubbling and the mashed potatoes are lightly browned, about 45 minutes. Let cool for 5 to 10 minutes before serving.

½ cup vegan butter, plus more for the baking dish

4 pounds Yukon Gold potatoes, peeled and cut into 1-inch pieces

Fine sea salt and freshly ground black pepper

1 cup plant-based milk, plus more if needed

2 tablespoons extra-virgin olive oil

1 yellow onion, finely chopped

2 carrots, peeled and finely diced

1 green zucchini, finely diced

1 yellow summer squash, finely diced

1 red bell pepper, seeded and finely chopped

1 yellow bell pepper, seeded and finely chopped

4 garlic cloves, finely chopped

1 cup tomato sauce

1 teaspoon finely chopped fresh thyme leaves

1 teaspoon cornstarch mixed with 2 tablespoons cold water

¼ cup vegan Worcestershire sauce

1 tablespoon white wine vinegar

★ BREWER'S FAVORITE ★

Originally crafted by our publisher **Sara Domville's** mother, Dorothy, this streamlined family-favorite recipe combines hoisin, soy sauce, rice vinegar, ginger, and sesame oil to create a magical potion that transforms ribs. Simply simmer the ribs in the sauce, toss them on the grill to crisp up, and dinner is served. The sauce is also terrific on grilled chicken, sausages, pork chops, and even a BLT sandwich. For the full experience, savor these ribs with warm, buttery garlic bread and a generous green salad, just as Sara's family does.

BABY BACK RIBS
WITH GINGER-HOISIN SAUCE

1½ cups ketchup

1 cup hoisin sauce

1 cup soy sauce

½ cup firmly packed dark brown sugar

1 yellow onion, quartered

4 garlic cloves, minced

¼ cup peeled and minced fresh ginger

½ cup rice vinegar

½ cup dry sherry

2 teaspoons toasted sesame oil

1 teaspoon red pepper flakes, or to taste

1 teaspoon freshly ground black pepper

2 racks pork baby back ribs, about 5 pounds total, cut crosswise into two-bone rib sections

To braise the ribs, in a large stockpot, combine the ketchup, hoisin sauce, soy sauce, sugar, onion, garlic, ginger, vinegar, sherry, sesame oil, red pepper flakes, and black pepper and stir to mix well. Add the ribs and stir until evenly coated. Cover the pot, place over medium-high heat, and bring to a gentle boil for 15 minutes. Reduce the heat to low and simmer, stirring occasionally, until the ribs are tender but not falling apart, about 1 hour.

Prepare a gas or charcoal grill for direct cooking over medium heat (400°F).

To reduce the sauce, when the ribs are ready, using tongs, transfer the ribs to a large sheet pan. Increase the heat on the stovetop to medium-high and bring the sauce to a boil. Adjust the heat to maintain a gentle boil and cook, stirring often, until the sauce is reduced to 2 to 3 cups, about 10 minutes. Remove and discard the onion pieces, then remove the sauce from the heat and keep warm.

To crisp the ribs on the grill, when the grill is ready, brush the grill grates clean. Add the ribs to the grill over direct heat, close the grill lid, and cook, turning occasionally, until nicely charred on both sides, about 10 minutes.

Slather the ribs with some of the sauce and continue to grill, turning once or twice, until sticky, 2 to 3 minutes longer. Transfer to a platter and serve with the remaining sauce alongside.

Makes 6 servings

Pairing great beer with great food is the mission of **Alisa Bowens-Mercado,** founder of **Rhythm Brewing Co.** in New Haven, Connecticut, the state's first Black woman–owned beer brand. This recipe for flank steak is the epitome of this focus. Beer, lime juice, garlic, and herbs are blended together to offer a tenderizing marinade for the steak. The robust flavors of this recipe are especially brought to life on the grill—with a beer in hand, of course. Warm Potato Salad with Beer Dressing (page 164) makes an excellent side.

FLANK STEAK WITH LAGER-LIME MARINADE

1½ cups Rhythm Brewing Unfiltered Lager, Rhythm Blue Unfiltered Light Lager, or other unfiltered lager

½ cup olive, avocado, or canola oil

½ cup fresh lime juice

4 garlic cloves, minced

2 tablespoons chopped fresh cilantro

1 tablespoon Worcestershire sauce

1 tablespoon kosher salt

1 teaspoon ground cumin

¼ teaspoon freshly ground black pepper

1 small jalapeño chile, sliced, or pinch of red pepper flakes (optional)

1 flank steak, about 2 pounds and at least ¾-inch thick

To marinate the steak, in a bowl, whisk together the lager, oil, lime juice, garlic, cilantro, Worcestershire sauce, salt, cumin, black pepper, and jalapeño chile (if using). Place the steak in a baking dish just large enough to hold it in a single layer. Using a sharp fork, poke the meat all over on both sides to help it absorb the marinade. Pour the marinade over the steak and turn the steak to coat well. Cover and marinate in the refrigerator for at least 6 hours or up to 10 hours.

When ready to cook, remove the steak from the refrigerator and let come to room temperature while you heat the grill.

Prepare a gas or charcoal grill for direct cooking over medium-high heat (400°F to 450°F). Remove the steak from the marinade and pat dry with paper towels.

To grill the steak, when the grill is ready, brush the grill grates clean. Add the steak to the grill over direct heat, close the grill lid, and cook, turning occasionally, until cooked to your liking, 8 to 10 minutes for medium-rare. Transfer to a plate and let rest for 10 minutes.

Cut the steak against the grain into ½-inch-thick slices and serve.

Only basic seasonings are needed here, as most of the flavor of this long-smoked beef roast comes from the wood smoke and a beer-and-broth spray used to keep the meat moist while it slowly cooks. This recipe from the **Geller family,** owners of the New Jersey–based **Three 3's Brewing Company,** makes great use of their Jersey Life Lager. Remember to spray the meat every hour while it's on the grill, and use a meat thermometer to monitor the progress. An extra can or two of the lager will help quench your thirst while you wait for the perfect bark to form on your roast. Serve with your favorite barbecue sides, like Southern Mac & Cheese (page 157), or Boston Lager Baked Beans (page 158).

SMOKED CHUCK ROAST WITH LAGER

To prepare for smoking, bring the roast to room temperature for 30 to 60 minutes. Set up a smoker for indirect cooking at low heat (225°F). Add a pan of water to the smoker. In a food-grade plastic spray bottle, combine ½ cup each of the lager and the broth. Pat the roast dry with paper towels.

To season the roast, in a small bowl, stir together the salt, granulated garlic, and pepper. Rub on the roast, pressing the seasoning evenly over the entire surface of the meat.

When the smoker is ready, place the roast, fat side up, directly on the grates and smoke for 3 hours. While the roast is smoking, spray it generously with the lager-broth mixture once every hour.

After 3 hours, in a sturdy grill-proof pan, spread the onion slices in an even layer and place the roast on top. Pour the remaining lager and broth over the roast along with anything remaining in the spray bottle.

Raise the smoker temperature to 250°F and cook the roast until an instant-read thermometer inserted into the center of the roast registers 165°F; you may notice a "stall" during which the temperature remains steady between 155°F and 165°F. This is normal when the connective tissue is breaking down, which helps create the tender meat we're after!

Once the internal temperature reaches 165°F, tightly cover the pan with heavy-duty aluminum foil. Continue cooking until the internal temperature reaches 200°F to 202°F. This can take another 2½ to 3½ hours. Every roast will be "done" at a different temperature. You're looking for your thermometer to slide easily into the roast.

Remove the pan from the smoker and place in a cooler. Pack the cooler with beach towels and let the roast rest for 30 minutes.

Transfer the roast to a cutting board and, using two forks, shred the meat. Scoop the meat onto a platter and moisten it with the cooking liquid. (Alternatively, skim the fat from the cooking liquid and then boil the liquid in a small saucepan until reduced by half to concentrate the flavors.)

1 boneless beef chuck roast, 4 to 5 pounds, trimmed of excess fat

1½ cups Jersey Life Lager or similar craft-brew corn lager

1½ cups beef broth

2 tablespoons kosher salt

2 tablespoons granulated garlic

1 tablespoon freshly ground pepper

2 yellow onions, sliced

JUDY & ROB NEFF, FOUNDERS OF CHECKERSPOT BREWING COMPANY

Judy and Rob Neff embarked on their brewing journey with the establishment of Checkerspot Brewing Company in Baltimore, Maryland, in 2018. Judy's fascination with craft beer had been ignited thirteen years earlier when she began homebrewing while pursuing her PhD in microbiology at Johns Hopkins University. What started as a hobby blossomed into a fervent passion. Meanwhile, Rob transitioned from his career as a civil engineer to join Judy on this entrepreneurial adventure, leveraging his expertise from operating Neff Rehabs construction company.

Over the initial five years, Checkerspot Brewing flourished, prompting Judy and Rob to seek out a permanent location for their brewery. Their search led them to a property near their original spot, conveniently close to downtown stadiums. It was during this pivotal time that they applied for the Brewing the American Dream program, recognizing its potential to propel their business forward. Their excitement reached new heights when they received the call announcing their victory in the 2022 Brewing the American Dream Brewer Experienceship competition, which coincided with the acquisition of their new property.

Throughout the design and construction phase, Checkerspot Brewing received invaluable guidance and support from the engineering and brewing group affiliated with the Boston Beer Company, transforming them from mere mentors to cherished friends. Grateful for the assistance and mentorship they received from the broader craft beer community, Judy and Rob are committed to paying it forward. They view Checkerspot Brewing not only as a brewery but also as a community hub, fostering connections through fundraising events, neighborhood gatherings, and celebrating life's milestones, like marriage proposals.

"AFTER FIVE YEARS IN BUSINESS, WINNING THE BREWING THE AMERICAN DREAM EXPERIENCESHIP PROVIDED INVALUABLE MENTORSHIP THAT HAS HELPED US GET TO THAT NEXT LEVEL, NOT ONLY TO GROW BUT ALSO TO CONTINUE OUR SUCCESS."

Judy & Rob Neff

The ethos at Checkerspot Brewing revolves around supporting the local community and celebrating the natural ingredients that contribute to crafting exceptional beer. Embodying the spirit of the Maryland state butterfly, the Baltimore checkerspot, Judy and Rob strive to uplift and empower their community while continuing their journey of growth and success.

This complete meal of grilled lamb chops, herb-roasted potatoes, and a simple arugula and celery root salad will take center stage at your next dinner party. **Judy and Rob Neff**, cofounders of **Checkerspot Brewing Company**, use their Juniperus IPA to infuse flavor into the lamb. Brewed with juniper berries, the hop-forward beer has piney undertones that enhance the flavor of the lamb. It also cuts through the richness of the duck fat in the potatoes, so be sure to pick up enough to serve with the meal. The homemade hop-infused vinegar in the salad dressing imparts a tangy and flavorful kick that complements earthy celery root, but feel free to substitute store-bought apple cider vinegar.

LAMB LOLLIPOPS WITH FINGERLING POTATOES & HOPPED-UP SALAD

Lamb Lollipops

2 racks of lamb, about 2 pounds each, frenched

Fine sea salt and freshly ground pepper

8 garlic cloves, minced

2 (16-ounce) cans Checkerspot Brewing Juniperus IPA or other IPA

2 tablespoons chopped fresh rosemary

2 teaspoons chopped fresh mint

¼ cup olive oil

Chopped fresh flat-leaf parsley, for garnish

Fingerling Potatoes

2 pounds fingerling potatoes, halved or quartered lengthwise

2 tablespoons melted duck fat or olive oil

2 tablespoons chopped fresh rosemary

4 garlic cloves, minced

Fine sea salt and freshly ground pepper

To marinate the lamb, season it all over with salt, then place in a baking dish just large enough to hold both racks. Sprinkle with half of the garlic and pour the beer over the lamb; it should be just submerged. Cover and refrigerate for at least 1 hour or up to overnight.

To season the chops, remove the lamb from the beer marinade, pat dry with paper towels, and cut into individual lamb chops. In a small bowl, stir together the rosemary, mint, remaining garlic, 1 teaspoon salt, and 2 teaspoons pepper. Add the oil and stir to combine. Arrange the lamb chops in a single layer on a sheet pan and rub the chops all over with the oil mixture, dividing it evenly. Set aside at room temperature for 30 minutes.

Make the potatoes while the lamb rests. Preheat the oven to 450°F. In a large ovenproof pan (preferably cast iron) with a lid, toss the potatoes with the duck fat, rosemary, garlic, and 1 teaspoon each salt and pepper. Cover, transfer to the oven, and cook the potatoes, turning them once or twice, until tender, about 20 minutes.

Make the salad and sear the lamb just before the potatoes are ready.

To make the salad (page 134), in a small bowl, whisk together the vinegar, lemon juice, garlic, salt, and pepper. While whisking constantly, slowly add the oil until the vinaigrette emulsifies. In a salad bowl, toss together the arugula and celery root. Drizzle with the vinaigrette and toss to coat evenly. Top with the feta and lemon (if using) and toss gently to mix well.

To cook the lamb chops, preheat a large cast-iron frying pan over medium-high heat. When the pan is hot, working in batches if needed to avoid crowding, add the lamb chops and cook, turning once, until nicely browned on both sides and done to your liking, about 6 minutes total for medium-rare.

continued...

...continued

Hopped Up Salad

2 tablespoons hop-infused vinegar (see Note) or apple cider vinegar

2 teaspoons fresh lemon juice

2 garlic cloves, minced

½ teaspoon fine sea salt

½ teaspoon freshly ground pepper

¼ cup extra-virgin olive oil

4 ounces baby arugula

½ celery root, peeled and shredded

1 cup (about 4 ounces) crumbled feta cheese

2 tablespoons thinly sliced preserved lemon (optional)

To serve, divide the salad and potatoes evenly among individual plates and arrange the lamb chops alongside, dividing them evenly. Sprinkle the chops with parsley and serve at once.

Note: You will need hop pellets to make hop-infused vinegar. We suggest Yakima Chief Hops Cryo Citra hop pellets, but feel free to try a different type. In a jar, combine 1 cup apple cider vinegar and 3.5 grams hop pellets. Cover and place in a dark spot at room temperature for at least 24 hours or up to 3 days. Once the vinegar has the flavor you like, strain it through a fine-mesh sieve and discard the hops. The vinegar will keep in a tightly capped jar in the refrigerator for up to 3 weeks.

★ BREWER'S FAVORITE ★

Finishing lobster on the grill adds just enough char to bring out its sweetness. Here, the succulent shellfish is enhanced by a tangy tomato vinaigrette, making each bite a celebration of flavors. The addition of malty Samuel Adams OctoberFest to the vinaigrette helps balance the richness of the buttery lobster meat.

GRILLED LOBSTER
WITH TOMATO VINAIGRETTE

To preboil the lobsters, bring a large pot three-fourths full of water to a boil over high heat and add 1 tablespoon salt. Plunge the lobsters head first into the water. Cover the pot and let the water return to a boil. Cook the lobsters until their shells begin to turn red, 7 to 8 minutes. Drain the lobsters and let sit until cool enough to handle. The lobsters will not be fully cooked at this point. They will finish cooking on the grill.

To prepare the lobsters, place a lobster belly side down on a cutting board. Insert the tip of a large, sharp knife into the center of the head, then cut downward lengthwise through the body, dividing the lobster into halves. Using the tip of the knife, remove and discard the dark intestinal tract running down the center. With lobster crackers or the back of a knife, crack the claws so the meat will be easy to extract. Set aside.

Prepare a gas or charcoal grill for direct cooking over medium heat (400°F).

To make the vinaigrette, in a medium bowl, whisk together 1 tablespoon of the honey, the ginger, vinegar, lime juice, sesame oil, and coriander seeds. Add the tomatoes, beer, and cilantro, stir gently, and season with salt and pepper.

To make the honey butter, in a small bowl, mash the butter with the remaining 4 tablespoons honey and the lemon juice, mixing well.

To grill the lobsters, when the grill is ready, brush the grill grates clean. Add the lobster halves, meat side up, to the grill over direct heat and cook, basting with the honey butter every couple of minutes, until the meat is fully cooked, 6 to 8 minutes. Serve the lobsters right off the grill with the tomato vinaigrette spooned over them or on the side.

Kosher salt and freshly ground pepper

6 live lobsters, about 1 pound each

5 tablespoons honey

2 teaspoons peeled and minced fresh ginger

2 teaspoons balsamic vinegar

2 teaspoons fresh lime juice

2 teaspoons toasted sesame oil

1 teaspoon cracked coriander seeds

1½ cups seeded and chopped tomatoes

½ cup Samuel Adams OctoberFest or Boston Lager

1 tablespoon chopped fresh cilantro

3 tablespoons unsalted butter, at room temperature

2 tablespoons fresh lemon juice

Dinner tonight is a trip to sun-splashed Jamaica with the island's famed jerk chicken at the center of a laid-back meal. **Conroy Outar and Alison Rosario** of **JA Patty,** based in Rhode Island, share this cherished recipe of whole chicken legs marinated in a spicy, aromatic blend and then grilled to smoky perfection. Serve these authentic flavors of the West Indies with rice and peas and fried sweet plantains plus a cooling beer to beat the spicy heat.

JAMAICAN JERK CHICKEN

To make the marinade, in a blender, combine all the ingredients except the chicken and pulse until well mixed into a paste that is not completely smooth; a few small chunks are okay.

To marinate the chicken, using the tip of a sharp knife, poke several small cuts into each chicken quarter. This will allow the marinade to penetrate the meat. Put the chicken quarters into a bowl large enough to hold the chicken and the marinade.

Pour the marinade over the chicken and then massage the marinade into each leg, including spreading it between the skin and the meat and making sure each leg is completely coated. Cover and refrigerate the chicken for at least 4 hours or preferably overnight.

Prepare a gas or charcoal grill for direct and indirect cooking over medium heat (375°F). Remove the chicken from the refrigerator and let sit at room temperature while the grill heats, about 20 minutes.

To grill the chicken, when the grill is ready, brush the grill grates clean. Remove the chicken from the marinade and discard the marinade. Place the chicken on the grill over direct heat, close the grill lid, and cook, turning occasionally, until nicely charred on both sides, about 10 minutes. Transfer the chicken to indirect heat, close the grill lid, and continue to cook until cooked through, 20 to 25 minutes. (An instant-read thermometer inserted into the thickest part of a thigh—not touching bone—should register 165°F.) Serve.

Leaves of 10 fresh thyme sprigs, roughly chopped

6 scallions, white and green parts, chopped

4 garlic cloves, chopped

2-inch piece fresh ginger, peeled and chopped, or ¼ teaspoon ground ginger

1 Scotch bonnet or habanero pepper, seeded and chopped

½ cup tomato paste

¼ cup olive oil

¼ cup JA Patty Tamarind Sauce & Dressing or tamarind chutney

¼ cup firmly packed light brown sugar

⅓ cup Worcestershire sauce

1 tablespoon dark molasses

1 tablespoon onion powder

2 teaspoons ground allspice

1 teaspoon liquid smoke

1 teaspoon kosher salt

½ teaspoon freshly ground black pepper

¼ teaspoon cayenne pepper

6 chicken leg quarters (drumstick and thigh), about 12 ounces each

This recipe from **Barry Bacon,** founder of **Spicy Water Distillery,** uses the company's Armory Village Vodka in a classic creamy tomato-based sauce. Choose your favorite twisted short pasta, such as radiatori or fusilli, and throw this dish together in less than a half hour. Delicious and versatile, it is fancy enough to impress weekend dinner guests and easy enough for a weeknight meal.

PASTA WITH CREAMY VODKA SAUCE

3 tablespoons unsalted butter

2 medium shallots, diced

2 garlic cloves, minced

¼ cup tomato paste

¼ teaspoon red pepper flakes, or more to taste

¼ cup Spicy Water Distillery Armory Village Vodka or vodka of your choice

1 (14½-ounce) can crushed tomatoes, with juices

1 teaspoon sugar

Kosher salt and freshly ground black pepper

12 ounces dried radiatori or fusilli pasta

½ cup heavy cream

⅓ cup grated Parmesan cheese

¼ cup shredded basil leaves

To make the sauce, in a large frying pan over medium-low heat, melt the butter. Add the shallots and garlic and cook, stirring occasionally, until tender, 4 to 5 minutes. Stir in the tomato paste and red pepper flakes until fragrant, about 1 minute. Working carefully, pour in the vodka and deglaze the pan, stirring to scrape up any browned bits from the pan bottom. Stir in the crushed tomatoes and their juices and the sugar, increase the heat to medium-high, and bring to a boil, stirring occasionally. Reduce the heat to low and simmer, stirring occasionally, until thickened, about 10 minutes.

To make the pasta, while the sauce is cooking, bring a large pot two-thirds full of salted water to a boil over high heat. Add the pasta and cook, stirring occasionally, until al dente, according to the package directions. Scoop out about 1 cup of the pasta cooking water, then drain the pasta.

To finish the pasta, add the cream and Parmesan to the sauce and heat, stirring, until smooth, about 2 minutes. Add the pasta and stir to combine. Add as much of the reserved pasta water, 1 tablespoon at a time, as needed to achieve a good balance of sauce and pasta. Season with salt and pepper.

To serve, transfer the pasta to a platter or shallow serving bowl and garnish with the basil. Serve at once.

★ BREWER'S FAVORITE ★

When pork shoulder cooks for hours, it becomes meltingly tender. Here, we simmer it slowly in plenty of beer and aromatics, then toss it with our favorite barbecue sauce. It's a great way to feed a crowd: just add a few side dishes, some bags of chips, and a cooler full of beer and you have a weekend party. Feel free to get creative with the barbecue sauce (try the sauce used on the Cheese Curd Burgers with Chili Sauce on page 94) or even with how you serve the pork. It's great piled high on toasted burger buns or makes a terrific topping along with lots of crunchy vegetables for a rice bowl too.

BEER-BRAISED PORK WITH BBQ SAUCE

1 boneless pork shoulder or Boston butt, about 6 pounds

2 (12-ounce) bottles Samuel Adams Chocolate Bock, Black Lager, or Cinnamon Roll Breakfast Bock

1 large yellow onion, roughly chopped

2 celery stalks, roughly chopped

3 bay leaves

2 whole allspice

10 peppercorns

1 tablespoon fine sea salt

2 cups favorite barbecue sauce

Put the pork shoulder into a large pot, pour in the beer, and then add just enough water to cover the pork. Add the onion, celery, bay leaves, allspice, peppercorns, and salt, place over high heat, and bring to a boil. Reduce the heat to a gentle simmer, cover with the lid ajar, and cook until the pork is very tender, 3 to 4 hours. (Alternatively, combine the same ingredients in a slow cooker and cook the pork on the high setting for 4 to 6 hours.)

Transfer the meat to a large cutting board. Strain the cooking liquid through a fine-mesh sieve set over a bowl and discard the solids. Skim off any fat from the liquid and set aside.

When the meat is cool enough to handle, shred it into bite-size pieces. Return the meat to the pot and add just enough of the reserved cooking liquid to moisten the meat. Taste and adjust the seasoning with salt if needed. Add the barbecue sauce and stir to mix well. Cover the pot and warm the pork over low heat, stirring occasionally, until hot. Serve warm.

★ BREWER'S FAVORITE ★

Jambalaya, rooted in Louisiana's Creole heritage, melds French, Spanish, and African culinary traditions. This version includes chaurice sausage, similar to Spanish chorizo, and features Samuel Adams Boston Lager for depth. If you can't find chaurice sausage, you can substitute andouille sausage. The dish boasts vibrant flavors of rice, tomatoes, and peppers, emblematic of the rich tapestry of Southern cuisine.

JAMBALAYA WITH SAUSAGE & BOSTON LAGER

To cook the vegetables, in a large skillet over medium-high heat, warm 3 tablespoons oil. Add the onion and cook, stirring, until transparent, about 5 minutes. Add the celery, bell peppers, garlic, half the parsley, and the pepper flakes (if using), and cook, stirring occasionally until fragrant and wilted, about 5 minutes.

Add the ham and sausage and cook, stirring, until lightly browned, about 5 minutes. Remove from heat and set aside.

To assemble and simmer the jambalaya, in a large heavy pot or Dutch oven over medium heat, warm the remaining 5 tablespoons oil. Add the uncooked rice and cook, stirring, until pale golden brown, about 5 minutes. Add the sausage-vegetable mixture along with the tomatoes, broth, and beer. Stir to combine. Cover and bring to a simmer, then reduce the heat to low and simmer gently for 20 minutes.

To cook the shrimp, lift the lid and quickly stir in the shrimp. Cover and continue to simmer until the shrimp is cooked through, about 15 minutes. Remove from heat and let stand, covered, for 10 minutes.

To serve, stir in the chopped scallions and remaining parsley. Serve at once, directly from the pot.

8 tablespoons olive oil
or avocado oil

2 large yellow onions,
coarsely chopped

5 celery stalks, coarsely chopped

1 red bell pepper, seeded
and coarsely chopped

1 green bell pepper, seeded
and coarsely chopped

5 garlic cloves, thinly sliced

1 cup chopped fresh flat-leaf
parsley

2 teaspoons crushed red pepper
flakes (optional)

⅔ pound smoked ham, trimmed
and cut into bite-sized pieces

1½ pounds smoked chaurice
or andouille sausage, cut into
bite-sized pieces

3 cups uncooked long-grain
white rice

4 large tomatoes, coarsely
chopped

4 cups chicken broth

½ cup Samuel Adams
Boston Lager

1 pound large shrimp,
shelled and deveined

14 thin scallions, white
and green parts, chopped

★ BREWER'S FAVORITE ★

Once you have marinated the shrimp, cooking them on the grill is a
quick and easy way to get dinner on the table. Plus, they come off the fire full
of flavor because of their long soak in our lager-based marinade. Serve the
shrimp on salad greens for a light lunch—check out the Big Green Salad with Hot
Pepper Vinaigrette (page 67)—or pair them with rice pilaf or pasta for a heartier
main dish. Or you can move them to the top of the menu for a great starter.

GRILLED SHRIMP WITH BEER & LEMON MARINADE

To marinate the shrimp, in a bowl, whisk together the beer, oil, lemon juice, garlic, scallions, basil, salt, and hot pepper sauce (if using). Add the shrimp and toss to coat evenly. Cover the bowl and marinate in the refrigerator for at least 2 hours or up to 8 hours.

If using bamboo skewers, soak in cold water for 30 minutes.

Prepare a gas or charcoal grill for direct cooking over medium-high heat (400°F to 450°F). Remove the shrimp from the marinade and discard the marinade. Thread the shrimp onto skewers, passing the skewer through the tail end and then the thick end of each shrimp.

To grill the shrimp kebabs, when the grill is ready, brush the grill grates clean. Add the kebabs to the grill over direct heat, close the grill lid, and cook, turning once, until the shrimp are pink and grill marked, about 5 minutes total. Transfer to a platter and serve.

⅔ cup Samuel Adams Boston Lager

½ cup olive oil

3 tablespoons fresh lemon juice

4 large garlic cloves, crushed

¼ cup finely chopped scallions, white and green parts

2 tablespoons chopped fresh basil leaves or 2 teaspoons dried basil

½ teaspoon fine sea salt

2 to 3 dashes of Louisiana hot pepper sauce (optional)

2 pounds large (31/40) shrimp, deveined with tail segment intact

Tangy from lemon and goat cheese, vegetable-laced orzo makes the ideal base for seared and then roasted salmon fillets. **Brian Neyenhouse,** founder of Massachusetts-based **Nutty Bird Granola,** created the dish, which is as delicious as it is versatile. The orzo can be served on its own as a light lunch. Or if salmon isn't your thing, top the pasta with Flank Steak with Lager-Lime Marinade (page 128) or Chicken Kebabs with Beer-Bourbon Marinade (page 121).

SUMMER ORZO WITH SALMON

4 tablespoons olive oil

½ yellow onion, finely chopped

½ bunch asparagus, ends trimmed and cut crosswise into 1-inch pieces

6 garlic cloves, minced

2 cups halved cherry tomatoes

1 pound dried orzo pasta

3½ cups low-sodium chicken or vegetable broth, plus more if needed

Fine sea salt and freshly ground pepper

5 ounces baby spinach, coarsely chopped

Finely grated zest and juice of 1 lemon

4 ounces fresh goat cheese

6 salmon fillets, each about 6 ounces, skinned and pin bones removed

Preheat the oven to 425°F.

To cook the vegetables, in a large saucepan over medium-high heat, warm 2 tablespoons of the oil. Add the onion, asparagus, and garlic and cook, stirring, until the onion is translucent, 2 to 3 minutes. Add the tomatoes and cook, stirring, until they soften, about 2 minutes.

Add the orzo and stir until coated with oil. Add the broth and 1 teaspoon salt and bring to a boil. Reduce the heat to medium-low and simmer, uncovered and stirring occasionally, until the pasta is al dente, 8 to 10 minutes. The liquid should be absorbed, but you can add more broth as needed to keep the mixture from drying out or drain off any excess liquid.

To finish the orzo, remove the pan from the heat, stir in the spinach and lemon zest and juice, and crumble the goat cheese over the top. Stir until well combined and the spinach has wilted. Season with salt and pepper. Cover to keep warm until serving.

To sear the salmon, while the orzo is cooking, generously season the salmon fillets all over with salt and pepper. Heat a large, well-seasoned ovenproof frying pan over high heat and add the remaining 2 tablespoons oil. When the oil is hot, add the salmon skinned side up and cook undisturbed until browned on the underside, about 2 minutes.

To finish the salmon, turn it skinned side down, transfer to the oven, and roast until it is just opaque and gives slightly when pressed, about 2 minutes.

To serve, divide the orzo mixture evenly among six dinner plates and top each portion with a salmon fillet, browned side up. Serve at once.

★ BREWER'S FAVORITE ★

This delightful pasta dish features eggplant, savory ham, fresh rosemary, and sweet peas, in a flavorful sauce made with Samuel Adams Boston Lager. The lager adds a rich depth of flavor that perfectly complements the ingredients and brings them all together. It's a satisfying and unique twist on classic pasta that will leave you wanting more.

PASTA WITH EGGPLANT, HAM & LAGER

Kosher salt, for the pasta water

1 pound penne

½ cup olive oil

1 small Italian eggplant (about 1 pound), peeled and diced

Fine sea salt and freshly ground black pepper

6 ounces smoked ham, trimmed and cut into ¼-inch cubes

1 cup Samuel Adams Boston Lager

1 teaspoon chopped fresh rosemary

1 cup fresh or frozen peas

Grated Parmesan cheese, for serving

To make the pasta, bring a large pot two-thirds full of salted water to a boil over high heat. Add the pasta and cook, stirring occasionally, until al dente, according to the package directions.

Make the sauce while the water heats and the pasta cooks. In a large frying pan over medium heat, warm the oil. Add the eggplant, season with sea salt and pepper, and cook, stirring often, until the eggplant is soft, about 10 minutes. Stir in the ham and cook, stirring, for 2 minutes. Add the lager and rosemary, increase the heat to medium-high, bring to a boil, and cook until the liquid is reduced by half, about 5 minutes. Stir in the peas, lower the heat to a gentle simmer, cover, and cook for 2 minutes.

To assemble and serve, when the pasta is ready, drain, add to the sauce, and cook, stirring, to coat well. Transfer to a serving bowl, sprinkle with plenty of Parmesan, and serve at once.

★ BREWER'S FAVORITE ★

A whole fish, gently steamed over porter-style beer and aromatic ginger, garlic, and lemongrass is an unforgettable experience. Served with sizzling ginger and thinly sliced garlic, this dish offers a harmonious blend of robust beer notes and fragrant flavors, promising a culinary experience that is both refined and satisfying.

GINGER STEAMED FISH WITH PORTER

To prep the fish, if using a whole fish, make a couple of shallow slits in the thick area of the fish on both sides. If using fish fillets, do the same. Measure the thickness of the fish at the thickest point. You will want to steam the fish for 10 minutes per inch of thickness.

To prepare the steamer with aromatics, in the bottom of a steamer or of a wok, combine the porter, sliced ginger, smashed garlic, and lemongrass.

To steam the fish, line a steamer rack or basket with cabbage leaves. Lay the fish on the leaves, place the rack or basket above the boiling liquid, and cover. Steam the fish according to the 10-minutes-per-inch rule. To check for doneness, slide a knife tip into the thickest part. The flesh should be opaque throughout.

Ready the garnish while the fish is steaming. In a small frying pan over medium heat, combine the sesame and peanut oils and heat until very hot. Remove from the heat, cover to keep hot, and set aside.

To assemble and serve the fish, when the fish is ready, carefully transfer it to warmed platter. Garnish the fish with the matchstick-cut ginger and garlic slices. Pour the hot oils evenly over fish and then sprinkle with the cilantro. Serve immediately.

1 whole fish, such as snapper or bass, 3 to 4 pounds, scaled and cleaned, or 2 pounds fish fillets

2 cups Samuel Adams Oaked Vanilla Porter or Black Lager

1-inch piece fresh ginger, peeled and sliced

3 large garlic cloves, lightly smashed

3 lemongrass stalks, root end and grassy tops discarded, tough outer layers peeled away, and tender stem chopped

Napa cabbage or large lettuce leaves, for lining steamer rack

Garnish

1 tablespoon toasted sesame oil

1 tablespoon peanut oil

2-inch piece fresh ginger, peeled and cut into fine matchsticks

2 garlic cloves, thinly sliced

½ cup fresh cilantro leaves

Harvested green, matoke bananas are a culinary staple in East Africa, particularly in Kenya, Uganda, and Tanzania. They are short and thick, rich in potassium and fiber, and always cooked before serving. Left to ripen, blackened matoke bananas are very sweet and soft. Here, **Charlette Lopez,** founder of the Kenyan-Mexican jam and sauce company **Jikonikwenu,** shares her unique recipe for the green fruits with njahi beans, white-striped black beans popular in Kenya. If you cannot find matoke bananas, you can substitute green plantains. Be sure to soak the njahi black beans overnight to ensure their tough skins soften during cooking. Dried kidney beans can be substituted for the njahi beans.

NJAHI BEANS MATOKE

11 green matoke bananas or 6 green plantains, unpeeled

1 cup black njahi beans (lablab beans), soaked overnight in salted water to cover

3 tablespoons olive oil

1 red onion, diced

1 teaspoon peeled and grated fresh ginger

1 garlic clove, minced

2 teaspoons curry powder

2 teaspoons adobo seasoning

2 teaspoons ground turmeric

1 teaspoon ground cumin

½ teaspoon ground cloves

1 teaspoon ground guajillo chile powder

Fine sea salt

1 (15-ounce) can tomato sauce

2 bay leaves

½ cup chopped fresh dill

8 cups water

½ cup chopped fresh cilantro

To prepare the bananas, cut off the top and end of each banana, leaving the remaining peel intact. In a pot, combine the bananas with water to cover and bring to a boil over high heat. Reduce the heat to medium and boil until tender, about 35 minutes. Transfer the bananas to a cutting board and let cool until they can be handled, about 15 minutes. Peel the bananas and discard the peels. Halve the bananas crosswise.

Meanwhile, drain and rinse the njahi beans. In a large saucepan, combine the beans with water to cover by 2 inches and bring to a boil over high heat. Reduce the heat to medium-high and boil gently until the beans are tender but not mushy, about 40 minutes. While the beans cook, skim off any scum that rises to the surface. Drain the beans in a fine-mesh sieve and set aside.

To cook the aromatics, in a large saucepan over medium heat, warm the oil. Add the onion and cook, stirring occasionally, until golden brown, about 10 minutes. Add the ginger, garlic, curry powder, adobo seasoning, turmeric, cumin, cloves, chile, and 1 teaspoon salt and cook, stirring, until fragrant, about 2 minutes.

Add the cooked beans, tomato sauce, bay leaves, dill, and water, cover, and bring to a simmer. Reduce the heat to low and simmer until the flavors come together, about 15 minutes.

Add the cooked bananas, stir to combine, and bring to a simmer. Reduce the heat to low and simmer until the bananas are soft, about 8 minutes.

To serve, using a wooden spoon, lightly mash everything in the pot. Taste and season with salt if needed, then scoop into a serving dish. Serve at once, garnished with the cilantro.

★ BREWER'S FAVORITE ★

Brining is a great way to ensure that the meat or poultry you are preparing
becomes flavorful and deliciously tender. This recipe uses dark beer—Samuel Adams,
of course—to infuse a subtle flavor that deepens the natural flavors of pork.
Patience is key, as the pork will need to sit in the brine for at least a day. But
after just one bite, you'll know the wait was worth it.

PORK TENDERLOIN WITH CITRUS-BEER BRINE

To make the brine, using a vegetable peeler, remove the peel from the orange
and the lemon and drop the peels into a saucepan. (Reserve the peeled
fruits for another use.) Add the beer, water, salt, sugar, peppercorns, fennel
seeds, and sage, place the pot over high heat, and bring the mixture to a boil.
Reduce the heat to low and simmer, stirring, until the salt and sugar dissolve,
then continue to simmer for 5 minutes longer to bring the flavors together.

Remove the brine from the heat, let cool to room temperature, and transfer
to a nonreactive container large enough to hold the brine and tenderloins.
Cover and refrigerate the brine until chilled, about 1 hour.

Add the tenderloins to the chilled brine and top them with a heavy plate
to keep them submerged. Re-cover the container and return it to the
refrigerator for at least 1 day or up to 3 days.

Remove the pork tenderloins from the brine, rinse under cold running water,
and pat dry with paper towels. Discard the brine.

Prepare a gas or charcoal grill for direct cooking over medium heat (400°F).

To grill the tenderloins, when the grill is ready, brush the grill grates clean.
Add the tenderloins to the grill over direct heat, close the grill lid, and cook,
turning frequently, until cooked to your liking, about 20 minutes for medium.
(An instant-read thermometer inserted into the thickest part of a tenderloin
should register 145°F.)

To serve, transfer the tenderloins to a cutting board and let rest for about
5 minutes. Cut into thick slices against the grain and serve right away.

1 orange

1 lemon

2 cups Samuel Adams Oaked
Vanilla Porter, Black Lager,
or other vanilla porter

2 cups water

½ cup kosher salt

¼ cup firmly packed light
brown sugar

2 teaspoons peppercorns

2 tablespoons crushed
fennel seeds

½ teaspoon dried sage

2 whole pork tenderloins, about
1 pound each, silver skin removed

Fascination with mead, an ancient alcoholic drink made from honey, and its connection to sustainability and beekeeping, led **Jeff Venuti** to found **Blisspoint Meadery** in Bedford, Massachusetts, where he produces a wide variety of high-quality meads for the modern palate. This recipe, which originally comes from Alsace, a region in northeastern France bordering Germany, is a family favorite that combines sauerkraut, pork ribs, and sausage with the sweet flavor of mead. The traditional honey-only semisweet mead he uses here provides a beautiful balance to the sourness of the sauerkraut. Or for an interesting twist, try one of Blisspoint's bourbon barrel–aged meads, such as Barreled Orchard or Barreled Home. Serve this bountiful main dish with a side of mashed potatoes.

CHOUCROUTE GARNIE

To prepare the sauerkraut mixture, in a slow cooker, combine the sauerkraut, mead, apples, garlic, peppercorns, and sugar. Stir to mix well.

To cook the bacon and onions, in a large frying pan over medium-high heat, cook the bacon and onions, stirring occasionally, until the onion is tender, about 6 minutes. Transfer the bacon-onion mixture to the slow cooker, leaving any fat in the pan. Stir the bacon-onion mixture into the sauerkraut mixture.

To brown the pork ribs, in the frying pan over medium-high heat, sear the ribs, turning once or twice, until nicely browned on both sides but not cooked through, about 4 minutes.

Arrange the ribs on top of the sauerkraut mixture. Cover and cook on the low setting until the rib meat pulls easily off the bone, 4 to 6 hours. Stir in the kielbasa, re-cover, and cook on the low setting for 1 hour longer.

To serve, spoon the sauerkraut mixture into shallow bowls, including some of the liquid. Top each portion with a rib and some of the sausages. Serve at once.

Note: Alternatively, to cook in a Dutch oven, cook the bacon and onions as instructed, then transfer to a plate. Brown the ribs as instructed, then transfer to another plate. Add the sauerkraut, mead, apples, garlic, peppercorns, sugar, and salt to the Dutch oven along with the bacon-onion mixture and stir to combine. Top with the ribs, cover, and bring to a boil over medium-high heat on the stovetop. Reduce the heat to low and simmer until the rib meat pulls easily off the bone, 2 to 3 hours. Add the kielbasa during the last hour of cooking. Serve as directed.

3 pounds sauerkraut, rinsed and drained

1 cup Blisspoint Meadery Sinensis mead or other semisweet or dry mead

2 tart-sweet apples, such as Granny Smith, peeled, cored, and diced

2 garlic cloves, crushed

8 peppercorns

2 tablespoons firmly packed light brown sugar

2 thick-cut bacon slices, chopped

2 yellow onions, chopped

6 country-style pork ribs

2 pounds kielbasa sausages, cut crosswise into ¼- to ½-inch slices

Substituting plantains for the more commonly used potatoes adds an inventive twist to pillowy gnocchi and offers a unique fusion of Caribbean and Italian culinary traditions. Chef **Ivo D'Aguiar,** owner of Florida-based **YALL Foods,** raises the game by pairing these sweet-savory dumplings with a rich brisket ragù. The result is a harmonious blend of flavors and textures that will delight your taste buds and leave you craving more. Feel free to substitute ripe fresh plantains, peeled and thickly cut on the diagonal, for the frozen plantains.

PLANTAIN GNOCCHI WITH BRISKET RAGÙ

Brisket Ragù

1 beef brisket, about 2 pounds, trimmed of excess fat

Kosher salt and freshly ground pepper

1½ cups vegetable, beef, or chicken broth

1 tablespoon canola or avocado oil

1 yellow onion, finely diced

2 carrots, peeled and finely diced

2 celery stalks, finely diced

3 garlic cloves, minced

1 cup dry red wine

1 tablespoon Worcestershire sauce (optional)

2½ cups canned crushed tomatoes

Plantain Gnocchi

1½ pounds frozen sliced sweet plantains

1¼ cups grated Parmesan cheese, plus more for serving

Kosher salt

1 cup all-purpose flour, plus more for dusting

3 tablespoons unsalted butter

To prepare the brisket, preheat the oven to 350°F. Season the brisket all over with salt and pepper, then place in a roasting pan just large enough to hold it. Pour the broth over the brisket. Cover the pan tightly with aluminum foil. Bake the brisket until it is very tender and easily pulls away from a fork, about 4 hours.

Transfer the brisket to a cutting board. Remove and discard any large pieces of fat, then shred the meat with two forks or chop into small pieces and set aside. Skim any fat from the cooking juices and reserve the juices.

To make the ragù, in a saucepan over medium heat, warm the oil. Add the onion, carrots, and celery and cook, stirring occasionally, until golden brown, about 5 minutes. Add the garlic and cook, stirring, until lightly golden, about 2 minutes. Add the reserved brisket and the cooking juices and stir to mix well. Pour in the wine and Worcestershire sauce (if using) and cook, stirring, until the liquid reduces almost completely, about 10 minutes. Stir in the tomatoes and bring the mixture to a boil. Reduce the heat to low and simmer for about 10 minutes to blend the flavors. Season with salt and pepper. Remove from heat, cover, and set aside.

To make the gnocchi, preheat the oven to 350°F. Line a large sheet pan with parchment paper, then spread the plantain slices in an even layer on the prepared pan.

Roast the plantain slices until soft when pierced with a fork, about 30 minutes. Let cool for a few minutes, then transfer to a blender and blend to a smooth puree. Transfer the puree to a wide, shallow bowl and let cool to room temperature, about 1 hour.

Add the Parmesan and 2 teaspoons salt to the plantain puree and stir until well mixed. Slowly stir in the flour, little by little, until the mixture becomes a soft, slightly sticky dough.

To form the gnocchi, lightly dust a sheet pan with flour. Divide the dough into quarters. Using your hands, roll each quarter into a rope ½ inch in diameter. Cut each rope crosswise into ¼-inch-wide pieces. Roll each piece on the back of fork tines to make the traditional gnocchi pattern, then transfer to the floured sheet pan.

Return the covered saucepan with the brisket ragù to low heat and gently rewarm, stirring occasionally.

To cook the gnocchi, bring a large pot of salted water to a boil over medium-high heat. Add the gnocchi to the boiling water, then reduce the heat to medium-low so the water is boiling gently. Cook the gnocchi until they start to float, about 5 minutes.

While the gnocchi are cooking, in a large sauté pan over medium heat, melt the butter. When the gnocchi are ready, using a slotted spoon, transfer the gnocchi to the sauté pan.

Toast the gnocchi in the butter, turning once, until golden brown on both sides, about 3 minutes total. Add half of the sauce to the pan and stir gently to coat the gnocchi with the sauce.

To serve, divide the gnocchi and sauce evenly between individual shallow serving bowls and top with the remaining sauce, dividing it evenly. Garnish each serving with Parmesan and serve.

SAVVY
SIDES

This signature Southern-style macaroni and cheese from **Devotis Lee** of **D Café & Catering** in Atlanta calls for eggs and a blend of creamy, flavorful cheeses—Cheddar, Provolone, and Gouda—in the sauce. She also uses plenty of white pepper, paprika, and yellow mustard powder to give the finished dish just the right spicy kick. Baked to golden perfection, this mac and cheese is more than a recipe—it's an experience.

SOUTHERN MAC & CHEESE

Preheat the oven to 350°F. Grease a 9 x 13-inch baking dish with butter.

To cook the macaroni, bring a large pot two-thirds full of salted water to a boil over high heat. Add the macaroni and cook, stirring occasionally, until about 1 minute shy of al dente, according to the package directions. Drain well, drizzle with a little oil, and toss to coat. Set aside.

To make the cheese sauce and assemble, in a large saucepan, whisk together the eggs, cheeses, 6 tablespoons butter, pepper, seasoning salt, paprika, and mustard powder. Place the saucepan over low heat and cook gently, stirring constantly, until the cheese has melted and the mixture is smooth. Be sure to keep the heat low so the eggs don't scramble. Add the cooked pasta to the pan and stir to coat evenly.

To bake the mac and cheese, pour the pasta mixture into the prepared baking dish. Pour the milk evenly over the top. Bake until bubbling and the top is golden brown, 35 to 40 minutes.

To serve, let rest for 5 minutes, then dig in and enjoy!

6 tablespoons unsalted butter, melted, plus room-temperature butter for the baking dish

Fine sea salt, for the pasta water

1 pound elbow macaroni

Olive oil, for drizzling

4 large eggs, lightly beaten

3 cups (about 12 ounces) mixed shredded cheeses, such as Cheddar, provolone, and Gouda cheese

1 tablespoon ground white pepper

2 teaspoons seasoning salt

1 teaspoon sweet paprika

1 teaspoon yellow mustard powder

3 cups whole milk

★ **BREWER'S FAVORITE** ★

Boston's beloved baked beans, made from scratch here with a healthy splash of Samuel Adams Boston Lager, are a perfect balance of salty-sweet, tangy, and rich. They are an ideal pairing with any grilled meats or hearty sandwiches. Try them with the Baby Back Ribs with Ginger-Hoisin Sauce (page 126), Smoked Chuck Roast with Lager (page 129), or Beer-Braised Pork with BBQ Sauce (page 140). This recipe yields a generous batch, perfect for gatherings.

BOSTON LAGER **BAKED BEANS**

2 cups dried navy beans

2 (12-ounce) bottles Samuel Adams Boston Lager

2 cups water

8 ounces sliced bacon, chopped

1 large yellow onion, finely chopped

¼ cup pure maple syrup

2 tablespoons firmly packed dark brown sugar

2 tablespoons yellow mustard powder

1 teaspoon fine sea salt

1 teaspoon freshly ground pepper

1 teaspoon sweet or smoked paprika

To soak the beans, pick over the beans and rinse well. Transfer to a bowl, cover generously with cold water, and let soak overnight.

To precook the beans, drain the beans, transfer to a large pot, and add 1 bottle of the beer and the water. The beans should be covered by about 1 inch of liquid. If they are not, add water as needed. Bring to a boil over high heat, then reduce the heat to low and simmer uncovered, stirring occasionally, until the beans are tender, about 1 hour.

Transfer the beans and their cooking liquid to a 9-inch square baking dish. Preheat the oven to 300°F.

Cook the bacon, in a frying pan over medium heat, stirring occasionally, until crisp, about 7 minutes. Using a slotted spoon, transfer to paper towels to drain. Pour off all but 2 tablespoons of the fat from the pan.

To make the sauce, return the pan to medium heat, add the onion, and cook, stirring occasionally, until deep golden brown, about 7 minutes. Add the maple syrup, sugar, mustard powder, salt, pepper, and paprika and stir to combine. Stir in the remaining bottle of beer and the cooked bacon. Bring the mixture to a simmer, then transfer to the baking dish with the beans and stir to mix well.

Bake the beans, uncovered, until the top is browned and the beans are very tender and flavorful, 45 to 60 minutes. Let sit for 5 minutes before serving.

KRISTINE CORTESE & DAVID WARNER,
COFOUNDERS OF CITY FEED AND SUPPLY

City Feed and Supply debuted in the vibrant Boston neighborhood of Jamaica Plain in 2000, marking the beginning of a community-driven culinary journey. Nestled at 66A Boylston Street, the inaugural location blossomed with the steadfast support of friends, family, and the local community. Cofounder Kristine Cortese envisioned a haven where neighbors could relish "a good cup of coffee and food you actually want to eat." Living in Jamaica Plain yet commuting to jobs outside the area, both Kristine and cofounder David Warner felt compelled to cultivate a business that would not only serve their community but also foster unity.

Drawing on their rural upbringing, where the local feed store served as a social hub, the duo was inspired by Kristine's grandfather's feed store, Cortese Feed and Supply, and David's childhood spent on a small farm. Thus, City Feed and Supply was born, an homage to the community-centric ethos of traditional country life.

Initially offering coffee and locally sourced groceries with an emphasis on wholesome foods, City Feed and Supply quickly evolved to include a full-service deli and café. The expansion continued in 2008 with the inauguration of a second location at the historic Masonic Temple building on Centre Street. With ample space and panoramic windows affording views of the bustling neighborhood, the new site facilitated an expanded menu, a wider array of groceries, and indoor seating, creating an inviting atmosphere for neighbors to connect.

"AS A PARTICIPANT IN BREWING THE AMERICAN DREAM, CITY FEED AND SUPPLY RECEIVED INVALUABLE SUPPORT FROM INDUSTRY EXPERTS THAT WE WOULD NOT OTHERWISE HAVE BEEN ABLE TO EASILY ACCESS. THEIR SUPPORT HELPED BUILD OUR BUSINESS TO WHERE IT IS TODAY."

Kristine Cortese & David Warner

Since its inception, City Feed and Supply has remained resolute in its commitment to build community through service. With a focus on locally sourced goods, award-winning sandwiches, organic fare, specialty groceries, and seasonal produce, it continues to be a treasured cornerstone of Jamaica Plain.

In the 1990s, a surplus of green tomatoes in his garden inspired a fellow named Tim to pickle them in sweet brine. Tim then gifted his friends **Kristine Cortese** and **David Warner** with a jar of the pickles, and they paired them with a New England sharp Cheddar, finding the flavor combination perfect. In 2002, when their company **City Feed and Supply** was creating its deli menu, that perfect combination became the Farmer's Lunch Sandwich, which, to this day, is one of its most popular offerings. Since its inception, City Feed and Supply has remained resolute in its commitment to "Build Community Through Service." With a focus on local goods, award-winning sandwiches, organic fare, specialty groceries,and seasonal produce, it continues to be a treasured cornerstone of Jamaica Plain.

PICKLED GREEN TOMATOES

2½ pounds hard green (unripe) tomatoes or tomatillos (husks removed and rinsed), cut into ⅛- to ¼-inch-thick slices

4½ cups distilled white vinegar

⅔ cup honey

5 teaspoons celery seeds

2½ teaspoons yellow mustard seeds

2½ teaspoons dill seeds

1 teaspoon peppercorns

3 garlic cloves, thinly sliced

Pack the sliced tomatoes into 4 sterilized pint-sized canning jars.

To make the brine, in a saucepan over medium-high heat, combine the vinegar, honey, celery seeds, mustard seeds, dill seeds, peppercorns, and garlic and bring to a boil, stirring until the honey has melted.

To pickle the tomatoes, remove the brine from the heat and ladle it over the tomatoes, submerging the tomatoes and leaving at least ½-inch headspace. (If you prefer fewer seeds in the jars, pass the brine through a fine-mesh sieve into the jars.)

Let the contents of the uncovered jars cool to room temperature. Cover the jars tightly and refrigerate for at least 2 hours before serving. The pickled tomatoes will keep in the refrigerator for up to 2 weeks. (Alternatively, you can use a water bath to can the tomatoes for shelf-stable storage; be sure to follow directions from a reputable source.)

★ BREWER'S FAVORITE ★

Germans have known for centuries that beer and potatoes make a great combination. This recipe unites these ingredients for a side dish that is sure to become a favorite. Gently mix the potatoes with the malty Boston Lager dressing while they are warm so they soak up the dressing (which is also excellent drizzled over roasted cauliflower or broccoli). To add meaty depth to the salad, mix in chopped crisp-cooked bacon or diced smoked sausages.

WARM POTATO SALAD WITH BEER DRESSING

Fine sea salt and freshly ground pepper

2½ pounds small red potatoes

¾ cup Samuel Adams Boston Lager

6 tablespoons extra-virgin olive oil

3 tablespoons apple cider vinegar

2 tablespoons country Dijon mustard

½ teaspoon sugar

½ small red onion, finely chopped

¼ cup finely chopped fresh flat-leaf parsley

2 tablespoons chopped fresh chives

To cook the potatoes, in a large pot, combine the potatoes with salted water to cover by 2 inches. Bring to a boil over medium-high heat, reduce the heat to medium, and boil gently until tender and a knife will slide into a potato with only a little resistance, about 20 minutes. Drain into a colander.

Make the dressing while the potatoes cook. In a glass jar with a lid, combine the beer, oil, vinegar, mustard, sugar, ½ teaspoon salt, and ¼ teaspoon pepper, cap tightly, and shake well. (Alternatively, whisk the ingredients together in a bowl.) Set aside.

To make the potato salad, when the potatoes are cool enough to handle, cut them into ½-inch-thick rounds. Transfer to a serving bowl and add the onion and parsley. Briefly shake the dressing to recombine, pour over the potatoes, and toss gently until the potatoes are evenly coated.

Taste and adjust the seasoning with salt and pepper if needed. Garnish with the chives and serve warm.

Makes 6 servings

In this colorful side, crunchy, slightly bitter red cabbage is slowly braised in a mix of apples, onion, apple cider, and cider vinegar, and, of course, Samuel Adams beer. Serve this good-for-you side—cabbage is loaded with antioxidants and vitamins—with meaty dishes, especially a succulent roast. Or you can put together a feast of hearty sides, partnering it with Sweet Potatoes with Hot Pepper Brown Butter (page 167) and Brussels Sprouts with Bacon & OctoberFest (page 170).

BRAISED RED CABBAGE WITH BEER & APPLES

To wilt the cabbage, in a Dutch oven or other large pot over medium heat, melt the butter. Add the cabbage and onion, cover, and cook, stirring occasionally, until the cabbage has wilted, about 10 minutes.

To braise the cabbage, stir in the apples, beer, cider, broth, vinegar, sugar, bay leaves, pepper, and caraway seeds and season with salt. Cook uncovered, stirring occasionally, until the cabbage is very tender, 30 to 45 minutes.

To serve, remove and discard the bay leaves, then taste and adjust the seasoning with salt if needed. Serve warm.

Note: To make this dish vegan, substitute 2 tablespoons olive oil for the butter and use vegetable broth.

4 tablespoons unsalted butter

1 medium red cabbage, cored and shredded

½ yellow onion, thinly sliced

2 cups peeled, cored, and grated Granny Smith apples

¾ cup Samuel Adams Black Lager, Oyster Stout, or Double Bock

½ cup apple cider

⅓ cup chicken or vegetable broth

2 tablespoons apple cider vinegar

1 tablespoon firmly packed light brown sugar

2 bay leaves

½ teaspoon freshly ground pepper

½ teaspoon caraway seeds

Fine sea salt

Makes 4 servings

Here, **Hillside Harvest** founder **Kamaal Jarrett** tops creamy baked orange-fleshed sweet potatoes (aka Garnet or Jewel yams) with a simple sauce of nutty browned butter and his tangy Hillside Harvest Original Hot Pepper Sauce. It couldn't be simpler, but the result is one that is both inspired and perfectly balanced. Serve these on their own with the Big Green Salad with Hot Pepper Vinaigrette (page 67) or with sausages and sautéed greens.

SWEET POTATOES WITH HOT PEPPER BROWN BUTTER

Preheat the oven to 400°F. Line a sheet pan with parchment paper.

To bake the sweet potatoes, prick them all over with the tines of a fork, then rub them evenly with the oil and a pinch of salt. Set the potatoes on the prepared sheet pan and roast until very tender and a fork easily slides into a potato with no resistance, about 45 minutes.

To make the brown butter, in a small saucepan over medium heat, melt the butter. Cook, swirling the pan, until the butter separates, foams, and turns light brown, 4 to 6 minutes. (The browned bits on the pan bottom should be about the same color as milk chocolate. That's where all the flavor is.) Remove the browned butter from the heat. Whisk in the pepper sauce and a pinch of salt.

To serve, transfer the cooked sweet potatoes to a serving plate. Slit each sweet potato lengthwise along the top and then use two forks to open it up a bit, exposing the flesh. Drizzle the spicy browned butter all over and inside the sweet potatoes, dividing it evenly. Garnish with the scallions and/or parsley, if you like. Serve warm.

4 medium-size orange-fleshed sweet potatoes, about 6 ounces each

1 tablespoon olive oil

Fine sea salt

3 tablespoons unsalted butter

2 tablespoons Hillside Harvest Original Hot Pepper Sauce or hot sauce of your choice

Thinly sliced scallions, white and green parts, and/or finely chopped fresh flat-leaf parsley, for garnish (optional)

Parboiling red potatoes, then "smashing" them on a sheet pan and baking them in the oven renders them crispy on the outside and creamy on the inside. The real magic comes from brushing them with olive oil and then sprinkling them with tasty, vegan-friendly Italian Herb Cashew Parm from **Alison Elliott's Farmer Foodie.** Be sure to select potatoes that are uniform in size so they cook evenly. If you don't have the Italian Herb Cashew Parm (you should!), you can use nutritional yeast as a substitute.

SMASHED POTATOES WITH "PARM"

1 pound small red potatoes

Fine sea salt, for the potato water

2 tablespoons extra-virgin olive oil

2 to 4 tablespoons Farmer Foodie Italian Herb Cashew Parm or nutritional yeast

Flaky sea salt, such as Maldon (optional)

To par-cook the potatoes, in a large pot, combine the potatoes with salted water to cover by 2 inches. Bring to a boil over medium-high heat, reduce the heat to medium, and boil gently until just fork tender, about 15 minutes. The timing depends on the size of the potatoes. Drain into a colander and let cool for 20 minutes.

Preheat the oven to 450°F.

To smash and season the potatoes, arrange the cooled potatoes in a single layer, well spaced, on a sheet pan. Using the bottom of a jar, smash each potato. Brush the potatoes with the oil and then sprinkle with Italian Herb Cashew Parm, adjusting the amount to suit your taste.

Bake the potatoes until browned, about 10 minutes. Turn on the broiler and broil until nicely crisped, 2 to 4 minutes. Sprinkle with flaky salt, if using, and serve at once.

Makes 4 servings

★ BREWER'S FAVORITE ★

Here is a great dish that's ready in a snap and uses only one pan. Slightly earthy and mildly bitter Brussels sprouts are thinly sliced and then quickly cooked with sweet onion and salty bacon. Serve this delicious cold-weather side with roasted pork or chicken.

BRUSSELS SPROUTS
WITH BACON & OCTOBERFEST

4 ounces sliced bacon, chopped

1 tablespoon olive oil

1 small yellow onion, thinly sliced

1 pound Brussels sprouts, trimmed and thinly sliced lengthwise

¼ cup Samuel Adams OctoberFest or Boston Lager

Fine sea salt and freshly ground pepper

Cook the bacon in a large frying pan over medium-high heat, stirring occasionally, until it begins to crisp, about 5 minutes. Pour off all but 1 tablespoon of the fat.

To cook the onion, return the pan to medium-high heat. Add the oil to the bacon fat along with the onion and cook, stirring often, until the onion has softened, about 5 minutes.

Add the sprouts and beer and season with salt and pepper. Cook, stirring, until most of the beer has been absorbed and the sprouts are just tender, 2 to 3 minutes. Serve warm.

While the roots of cornbread are found in Mesoamerican, Native American, and African cultures, this golden, tender version draws on Louisiana's longstanding cornbread tradition. Developed by **Cynthia Yette** of **Cynthia's Gumbo Express** in Chicago, it combines the mildly gritty texture of cornmeal with the richness of buttermilk and a healthy dose of sweetness. It is a welcome accompaniment to a bowl of spicy gumbo or makes a great standalone treat.

CLASSIC CORNBREAD

Preheat the oven to 425°F. Grease a 9-inch square baking pan with butter.

To make the batter, in a bowl, whisk together the cornmeal, flour, sugar, baking powder, and salt. In a second bowl, whisk together the buttermilk, egg, and the 4 tablespoons butter until blended. Add the buttermilk mixture to the cornmeal mixture and stir to mix well.

To bake the cornbread, pour the batter into the prepared pan. Bake until golden brown and a toothpick inserted into the center comes out clean, 20 to 25 minutes. Let cool for 5 minutes in the pan on a wire and then cut into squares and serve.

4 tablespoons unsalted butter, melted, plus room-temperature butter for the pan

1 cup fine yellow cornmeal

1 cup all-purpose flour

¾ cup sugar

4 teaspoons baking powder

½ teaspoon fine sea salt

1 cup buttermilk

1 large egg

These aren't your everyday roasted carrots. Created by Boston-based chef **Ken Oringer,** they are layered with complex flavors that make this side into dinner-party fare. First roasted in browned butter with plenty of herbs, the carrots are then glazed with rich, dark Samuel Adams beer. Once plated, they are drizzled with a curried yogurt-buttermilk dressing and topped with fresh herbs, orange zest, and dollops of spicy harissa. Try this same method with roasted winter squash or sweet potato spears.

BOCK-GLAZED CARROTS WITH YOGURT, HARISSA & HERBS

½ cup unsalted butter

2 pounds medium-size rainbow carrots or regular carrots, peeled

8 fresh sage leaves

1 fresh rosemary sprig

2 fresh thyme sprigs

1 bay leaf

Fine sea salt and freshly ground pepper

⅓ cup Samuel Adams Chocolate Bock, Cinnamon Roll Breakfast Bock, or Winter Lager

1 cup plain yogurt

½ cup buttermilk

3 teaspoons curry powder

5 fresh dill sprigs, chopped

1 tablespoon fresh lemon juice, or more if needed

¼ cup harissa sauce, for garnish

Finely grated orange zest, chopped fresh chives, and chopped fresh mint, for garnish

To make the browned butter, in a small saucepan over medium heat, melt the butter. Cook, swirling the pan, until the butter separates, foams, and turns light brown, 4 to 6 minutes. Remove the browned butter from the heat.

Preheat the oven to 425°F. Pile the carrots on a large sheet pan and drizzle evenly with the browned butter. Add the sage, rosemary, thyme, and bay leaf and toss to coat the carrots evenly with the butter and herbs. Spread the carrots in a single layer in the pan and season with salt and pepper.

Roast the carrots, turning and basting them with the butter, until just tender when pierced with a knife tip, about 30 minutes. Pour the beer into the pan and continuing roasting the carrots, turning occasionally, until tender and glazed, about 15 minutes.

Make the dressing while the carrots are roasting. In a small bowl, whisk together the yogurt, buttermilk, curry powder, dill, and lemon juice until smooth. Season to taste with salt, then taste and adjust the seasoning with more lemon juice if needed.

To assemble and serve, when the carrots are ready, remove from the oven and discard the sage, rosemary, thyme, and bay leaf. Transfer the carrots to a platter and drizzle the dressing evenly over them. Spoon dollops of harissa on top, garnish with orange zest, chives, and mint, and serve warm.

Colorful and packed with vegetables, this rice dish couples the heat of **Orisirisi Spice of Life** Rainbow Blend pepper sauce—created by **Ramon and Frances Hinds**—with the sweetness of coconut milk to create a symphony of flavors. Orisirisi Spice of Life is a family-owned gourmet pepper sauce company that takes pride in crafting a range of pepper sauces that elevate your favorite culinary creations. Hailing from diverse backgrounds, Ramon, a native of Trinidad and Tobago, and Frances, from Puerto Rico, form a dynamic husband-and-wife team. The rich tapestry of their respective cultures and the Caribbean flavors of their sauces result in extraordinary culinary experiences. Adjust the heat according to your preferences by adding more or less of the pepper sauce.

SPICY CALYPSO RICE

To cook the vegetables, in a saucepan over medium heat, warm the oil. Add the garlic and cook, stirring, for 1 minute. Add the carrot and cook, stirring, for 2 minutes. Add the chayote and cook, stirring, for 1 minute. Add the bell pepper and cook, stirring, for 1 minute.

To assemble and cook the rice, add the rice, broth, coconut milk, adobo seasoning, and pepper sauce and stir to mix well. Bring to a boil, cover, reduce the heat to low, and cook until the rice is tender and the liquid is absorbed, 25 to 30 minutes.

To serve, remove the pan from the heat and let sit, covered, for 10 minutes. Fluff the rice with a fork and serve warm.

2 tablespoons vegetable or other neutral oil

2 garlic cloves, minced

½ cup peeled, shredded carrot

½ cup peeled, julienned chayote

½ cup quartered, seeded, and thinly sliced red bell pepper

2 cups parboiled rice

3 cups vegetable broth

1 cup coconut milk

1 teaspoon adobo seasoning con pimiento (with pepper)

1 teaspoon Orisirisi Spice of Life Rainbow Blend pepper sauce or hot pepper sauce of your choice

★ BREWER'S FAVORITE ★

This unique dish marries the earthy notes of beer with the rich creaminess of Arborio rice, resulting in a comforting and flavorful Italian classic with a delightful twist. It is terrific served with roasted or braised meats, or keep it vegetarian and serve it with sautéed wild mushrooms or roasted vegetables, creating a versatile and satisfying meal.

RISOTTO WITH BEER & PARMESAN

6½ cups chicken broth

½ cup unsalted butter

2 yellow onions, finely chopped

1 teaspoon dried basil

1 teaspoon saffron threads, finely crushed

2 cups Arborio rice

1½ cups Samuel Adams Summer Ale or Boston Lager

Scant 2 cups grated Parmesan cheese

Kosher salt and freshly ground black pepper

First, warm the broth. In a saucepan over high heat, bring the broth to a boil. Remove from the heat, cover, and set aside.

To make the risotto, in a deep, heavy frying pan over medium heat, melt 4 tablespoons of the butter. When the foam subsides, add the onions, basil, and saffron and cook, stirring often, until the onions are translucent, about 5 minutes. Add the rice and stir until coated with the butter and heated through, 2 to 3 minutes. Pour in the beer and cook, stirring constantly, until almost fully absorbed.

Slowly start to add the broth: Adjust the heat to maintain a steady simmer, ladle in 1 cup of the hot broth, and cook, stirring frequently, until the rice absorbs most of the broth before ladling in another cup of broth. Continue in this fashion until all the broth has been added. When the rice begins absorbing the last addition of broth, add the remaining 4 tablespoons butter and the Parmesan and cook, stirring, until the rice is creamy but not wet. The total cooking time will be about 25 minutes.

To serve, season the risotto with salt and pepper and serve at once.

Makes 4 to 6 servings

★ BREWER'S FAVORITE ★

Beer-glazed onions offer a savory-sweet complement to any meal. Slowly cooked so the onions become caramelized, they are then glazed with dark beer to create robust depth. Serve over grilled or seared steaks for a natural pairing or on gourmet burgers for a boost of flavor. They also elevate vegetarian dishes like grilled portobello mushroom sandwiches or can be used as a topping for creamy mashed potatoes.

BEER-GLAZED ONIONS

To caramelize the onions, in a large sauté pan over medium heat, warm the oil. Add the onions, season with the salt, black pepper, and cayenne (if using), and stir and toss to mix well. Cook, stirring occasionally, until the onions are a golden caramel color, about 15 minutes.

To glaze the onions with beer, pour in the beer and cook, stirring, until glazed, 3 to 4 minutes. Serve hot.

4 tablespoons olive oil or unsalted butter

4 large yellow onions, sliced ¼ inch thick

½ teaspoon kosher salt

½ teaspoon freshly ground black pepper

Pinch of cayenne pepper (optional)

¼ cup Samuel Adams Oaked Vanilla Porter, Double Bock, or OctoberFest

The traditional rice bread of Liberia is gluten-free and banana-based and is made with cream of rice cereal instead of wheat flour. **Brigitte Harris,** founder of **Bridge's Kitchen,** which supplies traditional Liberian and West African food to the people of Staten Island, shares this recipe as a way to introduce others to one of Liberia's culinary classics. Be sure to bake the bread until it's quite dark brown, Brigitte advises. Don't worry—it isn't burned, she says. It's meant to be that color! Serve the bread plain or with butter and jam.

LIBERIAN **RICE BREAD**

Nonstick cooking spray, for the pan

2 cups cream of rice cereal

1 cup sugar

1 teaspoon baking soda

½ teaspoon fine sea salt

1 teaspoon freshly grated nutmeg

2 large eggs

1½ cups water

1 cup whole milk

¾ cup canola or avocado oil

2 teaspoons peeled and grated fresh ginger

1 teaspoon pure vanilla extract

4 ripe bananas, peeled and mashed

1 large ripe plantain, peeled and mashed

Preheat the oven to 350°F. Grease an 8 x 4-inch baking pan or two 12-cup standard muffin pans with cooking spray.

To make the bread batter, in a bowl, whisk together the cream of rice cereal, sugar, baking soda, salt, and nutmeg. In a food processor, combine the eggs, water, milk, oil, ginger, and vanilla and process until smooth. Add the rice cereal mixture and process until well mixed. Stop the processor and scrape down the sides of the bowl. Add the mashed bananas and plantain and process just until evenly mixed.

To bake the bread, scrape the mixture into the prepared pan or divide evenly among the prepared muffin cups. Bake the bread for 30 minutes or the muffins for 20 minutes, then reduce the oven temperature to 275°F and continue to bake until dark brown and cooked through and a toothpick inserted into the center of the bread comes out clean, about 30 minutes longer for the breads, or 15 minutes longer for the muffins.

Let cool in the pan(s) on a wire rack for 10 minutes, then turn the bread(s) out of the pan(s) onto the rack. Serve warm or at room temperature.

Embrace the warmth of family tradition with this cherished beer bread recipe from **Betty Bollas,** cofounder of the majority woman-owned **Fibonacci Brewing Company,** located in the small town of Mount Healthy, near Cincinnati. More than just bread, this recipe, which uses the company's In Honor Of light lager, weaves together love and self-sustainability. Each slice is a tribute to the influential women in our lives.

NANA'S **BEER BREAD**

Preheat the oven to 350°F. Lightly grease a 9 x 5-inch loaf pan with butter or spray with cooking spray.

To make the bread batter, in a large bowl, whisk together the flour, sugar, and salt. Slowly add the beer to the flour mixture while gently stirring just until combined. Be careful not to overmix; the batter should be slightly lumpy.

Transfer the batter to the prepared pan and smooth the top with a rubber spatula. Drizzle the butter evenly over the top of the batter. This will give your bread a beautiful golden, crispy crust.

Bake the bread until the top is golden brown and a toothpick inserted into the center of the loaf comes out clean, about 1 hour.

Let cool in the pan on a wire rack for 10 to 15 minutes, then turn the bread out of the pan onto the rack, turn the bread upright, and let cool completely before slicing.

Unsalted butter or nonstick cooking spray, for the pan

3 cups self-rising flour

3 tablespoons sugar

Pinch of fine sea salt

¾ cup In Honor Of light lager or other light lager, at room temperature

2 tablespoons unsalted butter, melted

These light and fluffy yeasted biscuits get a modern twist with the addition of everything bagel seasoning. The recipe, crafted by **Tiffani Neal** of Atlanta-based **Barlow's Foods,** uses her three-in-one pancake, biscuit, and waffle mix as the biscuit base, making these biscuits both easy and convenient. Of course, if everything bagel seasoning isn't your thing, just leave it off. And if you don't have access to her innovative mix, you can swap it out for another biscuit, pancake, and waffle mix.

EVERYTHING **ANGEL BISCUITS**

1 envelope (2¼ teaspoons) active dry yeast

¼ cup warm water (105°F to 110°F)

3 cups Barlow's Original Pancake, Biscuit & Waffle Mix

½ cup cold unsalted butter, cut into small pieces, plus more for serving

1 cup buttermilk

All-purpose flour, for dusting

Topping

2 tablespoons unsalted butter, melted, for brushing

¼ cup everything bagel seasoning

To activate the yeast, in a small bowl, stir the yeast into the warm water. Set aside until foamy, 5 to 10 minutes.

To make the dough, put the pancake mix into a large bowl and scatter the butter over the top. Using your fingers or a pastry blender, work the butter into the pancake mix until the mixture looks like large breadcrumbs. Add the buttermilk and yeast mixture and stir just until combined. The dough will be soft.

To roll and cut the biscuits, line a sheet pan with parchment paper. Dust a work surface with flour and turn the dough out onto it. Knead gently a few times just until the dough comes together. Using your hands, pat the dough in a rectangle about ½ inch thick (or roll out with a rolling pin). Using a 2-inch round biscuit cutter, cut out as many rounds as possible from the dough. Transfer them to the prepared sheet pan, spacing them about 2 inches apart. Gather up the dough scraps, press together gently, pat out ½ inch thick, cut out more biscuits, and add to the pan.

Let the biscuits rise until slightly puffy, 20 to 30 minutes.

To bake the biscuits, preheat the oven to 425°F. Bake the biscuits until the tops are golden brown, 12 to 15 minutes.

Immediately brush the tops with butter and sprinkle with the everything bagel seasoning.

Let the biscuits cool in the pan on a wire rack for a few minutes, then serve warm with plenty of butter.

DYNAMIC
DESSERTS & DRINKS

Calling all coffee lovers! These delectable cookies come from **Brewpoint Coffee** founder **Melissa Villanueva,** who champions connection and community through her coffee shop and roastery in Elmhurst, Illinois. If you can't get your hands on The Acrobat, her nutty, caramelly medium roast made from a blend of Costa Rican and Mexican beans, any high-quality medium roast will do. Quick and straightforward to make, the hardest part of this recipe is resisting taking a bite until the cookies have cooled.

TOFFEE COFFEE **COOKIES**

Preheat the oven to 350°F. Generously grease a large sheet pan with butter.

To make the cookie dough, in a medium bowl, whisk together the flour, coffee, and baking powder. In a large bowl, using an electric mixer, beat together the ½ cup butter, sugar, syrup, egg, and vanilla on medium-high speed until the mixture is smooth and creamy, about 2 minutes. Gradually add the flour mixture to the butter mixture, beating on low speed until thoroughly incorporated. Gently fold in the toffee chips just until evenly distributed throughout the dough.

To roll the cookies, spread a little cinnamon in a small, shallow bowl. Scoop out about 2 tablespoons of the dough and roll between your palms into a ball about 1½ inches in diameter. Roll the ball in the cinnamon, coating evenly, and set on the prepared sheet pan. Repeat with the remaining dough, spacing the balls about 2 inches apart.

Gently flatten each ball into a ½-inch-thick disk, then lightly brush each dough disk with the syrup.

Bake the cookies until the edges are golden brown but the middle is still pale but set, about 10 minutes. Let cool in the pan on a wire rack for a few minutes, then transfer the cookies to the rack and let cool completely before serving. The cookies will keep in an airtight container at room temperature for up to 4 days.

½ cup unsalted butter, at room temperature, plus more for the pan

2 cups all-purpose flour

2 tablespoons Brewpoint Coffee's The Acrobat medium-roast ground coffee

1 teaspoon baking powder

1 cup sugar

¼ cup toffee-flavored syrup, plus more for brushing

1 large egg

1 teaspoon pure vanilla extract

1 cup toffee bits, preferably Heath brand

Ground cinnamon, for rolling

Tucked secretly inside each of these rich, dark chocolate cookies is a gooey marshmallow, making them an ideal sweet for a fireside evening. You'd never even guess that these cookies, from **Maya Madsen,** founder and CEO of **Maya's Cookies,** are vegan. She started her top-tier Black-owned gourmet vegan cookie company in San Diego, California, when she couldn't find vegan treats to satisfy her sweet tooth. Maya suggests pairing this riff on the campout classic with a creamy stout. Be sure to refrigerate the dough for at least 3 hours, and once the marshmallows are added, the dough cannot go back into the refrigerator.

VEGAN S'MORES COOKIES

1½ teaspoons vegan egg replacer, such as Ener-G brand

2 tablespoons water

¾ cup nondairy butter, at room temperature

½ cup firmly packed light brown sugar

½ cup granulated sugar

1 tablespoon pure vanilla extract

1½ cups all-purpose flour

¼ cup raw cacao powder

1 teaspoon baking soda

½ teaspoon fine sea salt

½ cup coarsely chopped vegan semisweet chocolate, in ¼-inch chunks

12 vegan marshmallows, such as Dandies brand

To mix the wet ingredients, in a small bowl, whisk together the egg replacer powder and water until frothy. In a medium bowl, whisk together the butter, both sugars, and vanilla until creamy. Add the egg-replacer mixture to the butter mixture and whisk until fully incorporated.

To mix the dry ingredients, in a large bowl, whisk together the flour, cacao powder, baking soda, and salt.

To make the dough, pour the wet ingredients into the flour mixture and stir until the ingredients are just combined and no dry spots are visible. Stir in the chocolate and mix until evenly distributed throughout the dough. Cover the bowl and refrigerate for at least 3 hours or up to overnight.

Remove the dough from the refrigerator. If the dough was chilled for longer than 3 hours, let it sit at room temperature for about 15 minutes. This makes it easier to scoop and mold.

Position two oven racks in the center of the oven and preheat the oven to 350°F. Line two sheet pans with parchment paper.

To assemble the cookies, using a 3-tablespoon cookie scoop, scoop up a heaping ball of dough. With the dough in the scoop, use your thumb to poke a hole in the dough ball that reaches to the bottom.

Stuff a marshmallow into the hole, squishing and pressing it all the way into the scoop. Make sure the marshmallow is not peeking over the top edge of the scoop. Seal the hole closed with dough, then release the dough ball onto a prepared sheet pan. Repeat to make 12 cookies, dividing them between the pans and spacing them 2 inches apart.

Bake the cookies, switching the pans between the racks and rotating them back to front at the halfway point, until the cookies are cracked and the marshmallows start to puff up and expand, 13 to 15 minutes. Let cool in the pans on wire racks for 5 minutes, then transfer the cookies to the racks and let cool completely before serving.

HEATHER HIGGINS YUNGER, FOUNDER OF TOP SHELF COOKIES

A fervent Boston hockey fan with a penchant for superstition, Heather Higgins Yunger concocted her famed recipe for Black & Gold cookies during the 2010–2011 National Hockey League season. These tempting treats fused rich dark chocolate with crunchy peanut butter chips. Heather's ritual of sharing these cookies with friends before every game seemed to bring good luck, as her team ultimately clinched the championship title. Among her ardent supporters was Samuel Adams Brewer and Director of Partnerships Jennifer Glanville Love, whom Heather met at a hockey game. Jennifer, together with Heather's father, encouraged Heather to pursue her passion for cookies. She took their advice to heart and founded Top Shelf Cookies in 2014, operating out of a shared kitchen in Boston. Her commitment to quality ingredients and innovative flavors quickly earned her the title of Boston's Best Cookies.

When Jennifer approached Heather with the idea of creating a custom Samuel Adams Boston Lager cookie, she readily embraced the challenge. Despite facing setbacks, including an unsuccessful pitch at the Brewing the American Dream competition in 2016, Heather persisted. She applied again in 2019, and this time emerged as a finalist, eventually securing the grant. This funding proved instrumental in navigating the challenges posed by the COVID-19 pandemic. By strategically investing the capital in her online channels, Heather strengthened Top Shelf Cookies' resilience and moved closer to her dream of opening the company's first storefront in the Boston neighborhood of Dorchester, where she grew up.

"BREWING THE AMERICAN DREAM HAS MADE ALL THE DIFFERENCE FOR US. IT'S GOOD TO KNOW SOMEONE HAS YOUR BACK AND UNDERSTANDS IT'S HARD TO KNOW HOW TO DO EVERYTHING."

Heather Higgins Yunger

Despite the rigors of entrepreneurship, Heather considers herself blessed to helm a cookie business that brings joy to her customers and herself. From experimenting with unique ingredients to paying homage to her hometown of Boston through her creations, Heather's journey with Top Shelf Cookies epitomizes her passion for baking and community engagement. As she continues to expand her business and serve her community, Heather remains steadfast in her commitment to delivering cookies as fresh and interesting as the city they hail from.

At both work and home, Heather is accompanied by her faithful companion, Lola, who holds the esteemed title of CDO (Chief Dog Officer) at Top Shelf Cookies. Although she may not participate in business meetings, Lola is a cherished member of the team and Heather's closest confidant. Adopted in 2022 shortly after the launch of Top Shelf Cookies, Lola takes her role seriously, diligently sniffing out any unsecured cookies in Heather's house.

When **Heather Higgins Yunger**, the mastermind behind **Top Shelf Cookies**, crafted a heavenly oatmeal chocolate chunk cookie, she sought her community's input for a suitable name in the form of a contest. The winning moniker was OFD—Oaty, Fudgy, Delicious—and the winner generously donated the prize money to a local health center in gratitude for its workers tireless efforts during the COVID-19 pandemic. With plenty of local Dorchester pride, Heather shares the OFD cookie recipe here. It truly does live up to its name!

"OFD" COOKIES

1½ cups all-purpose flour

½ teaspoon baking powder

½ teaspoon fine sea salt

1 cup unsalted butter, at room temperature

1 cup granulated sugar

1 cup firmly packed light brown sugar

2 large eggs

3 cups old-fashioned rolled oats

2 cups dark chocolate chunks

Position two oven racks in the center of the oven and preheat the oven to 350°F. Line two sheet pans with parchment paper.

To make the cookie dough, in a medium bowl, whisk together the flour, baking powder, and salt. In a large bowl, using an electric mixer, beat together the butter and both sugars on medium-high speed until light and fluffy, about 2 minutes. Add the eggs one at a time, beating after each addition just until incorporated. With the mixer on low speed, slowly add the flour mixture, beating until incorporated. Add the oats and chocolate chunks and beat just until evenly mixed. The dough will be stiff.

Using a 4-tablespoon cookie scoop, scoop up balls of dough and arrange them on the prepared sheet pans, placing 8 or 9 balls on each pan and spacing them evenly.

Bake the cookies, switching the pans between the racks and rotating them back to front at the halfway point, until golden brown, about 11 minutes. Let cool in the pans on wire racks for 5 minutes, then transfer the cookies to the racks and let cool completely before serving. The cookies will keep in an airtight container at room temperature for up to 4 days.

Sweet Tahini founder **Hila Krikov** grew up eating sesame candies and tahini-based sweets like halvah. Her mom's tahini cookies were a particular favorite, and she remembers her baking them in the 1980s from pantry staples. If you're unfamiliar with whole-grain spelt flour and date molasses, this a great opportunity to explore new ingredients and use them to make other Middle Eastern–inspired dishes. These cookies are soft in texture and have a buttery flavor—even though there is no butter in these vegan treats!

TAHINI SPELT COOKIES

1¾ cups whole spelt flour

¼ cup sugar

1½ teaspoons baking powder

¼ teaspoon fine sea salt

1 cup tahini paste

¼ cup coconut oil

3 tablespoons sesame seeds

2 tablespoons date molasses, honey, or pure maple syrup

Preheat the oven to 350°F. Line a sheet pan with parchment paper.

To make the dough, in the bowl of a stand mixer fitted with the dough hook, mix together the spelt flour, sugar, baking powder, and salt on low speed. Add the tahini, coconut oil, sesame seeds, and date molasses to the bowl, and beat on low speed until the ingredients come together and a soft, uniform dough forms.

To form the cookies, scoop up a scant 2 tablespoons of the dough, roll between your palms into a ball 1½ inches in diameter, and place on the prepared sheet pan. Repeat with the remaining dough, spacing the balls about 1 inch apart. Using the tines of a fork, flatten each ball into a ½-inch-thick disk.

Bake the cookies until pale and still soft, 8 to 9 minutes. Do not overbake! Let cool in the pan on a wire rack until firm before serving. The cookies will keep in an airtight container at room temperature for up to 1 week.

Makes 18 bars

Briana Azier, founder of Massachusetts-based **Bri's Sweet Treats,** is a master of layering textures and flavors in her irresistible line of artisanal chocolate creations. Here, just three ingredients—almond-studded dark chocolate, creamy peanut butter, and graham crackers—come together quickly for an unforgettable solution to a craving for something sweet. Pair these bars with a robust stout.

CHOCOLATE BARS WITH PEANUT BUTTER & GRAHAMS

Line the bottom and sides of a 9 x 13-inch baking pan with parchment paper.

Gently melt half the almond bark in a small saucepan over low heat, stirring occasionally, until the chocolate is smooth. (Alternatively, put half of the almond bark in a microwave-safe bowl and microwave on high power for 20-second bursts, stirring after each burst, until the chocolate is melted and smooth.)

Pour the melted almond bark into the prepared pan and, using an offset spatula or other thin metal spatula, spread it in a thin, even layer. Let sit until hardened. To speed up the process, put the pan into the refrigerator for 5 to 10 minutes.

Once the almond bark is set, dollop the peanut butter evenly over it. Then, using the spatula, spread it in an even layer, covering the entire surface of the almond bark.

Arrange the graham crackers in a single layer over the peanut butter, covering it completely.

Melt the remaining almond bark the same way you melted the first half. Pour the melted almond bark over the graham cracker layer, smoothing it into a thin, even layer and covering the crackers completely.

Let sit until the almond bark hardens, then cut into pieces and serve.

1½ pounds store-bought chocolate almond bark, broken into pieces

1½ cups (12 ounces) creamy peanut butter

9 whole graham cracker sheets

Makes 2 pints ice cream; enough for 8 floats

★ BREWER'S FAVORITE ★

This creative twist on the classic ice cream float combines the bold flavors of Samuel Adams Black Lager with ultra-creamy mascarpone ice cream. The rich, malty flavors of the dark beer blends well with the sweet ice cream for a unique and memorable experience. To really take these over the top, fill mini chocolate chip cookies with small scoops of the ice cream and serve them alongside the floats.

BLACK LAGER FLOATS
WITH MASCARPONE ICE CREAM

To make the mascarpone ice cream, fill a large bowl with ice cubes and water. In a saucepan, combine the cream, mascarpone cheese, and half of the sugar. Using the back of a paring knife, scrape the seeds from the vanilla bean pod and add the seeds and pod to the cream mixture. Bring the mixture to a gentle boil over medium heat, stirring until smooth. Remove from the heat.

In a heatproof bowl, whisk together the whole eggs, egg yolks, the remaining sugar, and the salt. While whisking constantly, slowly pour the hot cream mixture into the egg mixture, continuing to whisk until well blended. Strain the mixture through a fine-mesh sieve into a medium bowl and rest the bowl in the ice bath. Let the ice cream base cool, stirring occasionally, until well chilled.

Pour the chilled ice cream base into an ice cream maker and freeze according to the manufacturer's instructions. Transfer to an airtight container and place in the freezer until firm, at least 2 hours. It will keep for up to 2 weeks.

For each float, in a pint or pilsner glass, add 2 small scoops of the mascarpone ice cream. Slowly pour in 1 cup of the beer. Repeat to make as many floats as desired.

2 cups heavy cream

2 cups mascarpone cheese

1 cup sugar

1 vanilla bean, split lengthwise

3 large whole eggs

7 large egg yolks

1 teaspoon fine sea salt

1 cup Samuel Adams Black Lager, Double Bock, or Cinnamon Roll Breakfast Bock

When **Mariana Cortez,** founder of **Bunnie Cakes** in Miami, Florida, started her plant-based baking business, she based it on three principles: compassion for animals, inclusion of everyone regardless of dietary restriction, and a passion to realize her dream. She makes these delicious and easy doughnuts in a pan with heart-shaped wells, but a standard doughnut pan also works great. And they taste so good that no one will believe they're vegan. The addition of applesauce to the batter keeps the doughnuts moist and also adds natural sweetness. Personalize them with sprinkles in your favorite color.

VEGAN CHOCOLATE CAKE **DOUGHNUTS**

4 tablespoons coconut oil, melted, or canola or other neutral oil, plus more for the pan

1 cup all-purpose flour

½ cup sugar

¼ cup unsweetened natural cocoa powder

½ teaspoon baking soda

½ teaspoon baking powder

¼ teaspoon fine sea salt

½ cup unsweetened almond milk or other plant-based milk

¼ cup unsweetened applesauce

1 teaspoon pure vanilla extract

½ cup vegan chocolate chips

Vegan sprinkles, chopped chocolate, and/or cocoa nibs, for decorating (optional)

Preheat the oven to 350°F. Grease two 6-well standard doughnut pans with heart-shaped or round wells with oil.

To make the batter, in a bowl, whisk together the flour, sugar, cocoa powder, baking soda, baking powder, and salt. In a separate bowl, whisk together the almond milk, applesauce, 2 tablespoons of the coconut oil, and the vanilla. Pour the milk mixture into the flour mixture and stir just until evenly mixed. Be careful not to overmix.

Spoon the batter into a piping bag fitted with a large round tip and pipe the batter into the prepared pan, dividing the batter evenly. (Alternatively, spoon the batter into the prepared pan.)

Bake the doughnuts until puffed and cooked through, 10 to 13 minutes. Let cool in the pan on a wire rack for 5 minutes, then turn the doughnuts out onto the rack and let cool completely.

To make the glaze, in a small, microwave-safe bowl, combine the chocolate chips and the remaining 2 tablespoons oil. Microwave the mixture on high power in 20-second bursts, stirring after each burst, until the chocolate is melted and the mixture is smooth. (Alternatively, combine the chocolate chips and the remaining 2 tablespoons oil in a small saucepan and warm over low heat, stirring occasionally, until the chocolate is melted and smooth.)

To glaze the doughnuts, dip a cooled doughnut, top side down, into the warm chocolate, covering the top completely, then place right side up on the wire rack.

To decorate, top the glaze immediately with sprinkles, chopped chocolate, and/or cocoa nibs, if using. Repeat with the remaining doughnuts. Let the glaze set before serving.

BREWING THE
AMERICAN DREAM
Winner
Hopkinsville
Brewing
Company

KATE RUSSELL, FOUNDER AND CO-OWNER OF HOPKINSVILLE BREWING COMPANY

After leaving the US Army in 2006, Kate Russell transitioned into the role of a stay-at-home mom until her then husband expressed his desire to open a brewery. Initially reluctant, she unexpectedly found herself drawn to the world of beer and brewing, opting to continue with the brewery venture following their divorce.

In 2016, Kate founded the Hopkinsville Brewing Company, marking the advent of craft beer brewing in Christian County, Kentucky. Situated in a struggling downtown area, her vision was to contribute to local revitalization efforts while introducing locally crafted beer to the community. Her partner and co-owner, Joey Medieros, was originally an enthusiastic homebrewer and, like Kate, had retired from the army. He pursued a formal brewing education before joining the brewery in 2017, where they have been brewing together ever since.

Emphasizing community engagement, the Hopkinsville Brewing Company taproom regularly hosts talks organized by the area's library and museum, while the company's beer names pay homage to local attractions or personalities, such as the Bell Witch Baltic Porter, inspired by regional folklore.

In 2021, Hopkinsville Brewing received the Brewing the American Dream Brewer Experienceship award. It came at an opportune moment, as Kate and Joey were coping with the initial stages of their brewery's expansion while grappling with the logistics of scaling up production and managing the

"OUR INVOLVEMENT WITH BREWING THE AMERICAN DREAM WAS SERENDIPITOUS. IT WAS SPARKED BY A LAST-MINUTE DECISION TO APPLY THAT WAS PROMPTED BY A SOCIAL MEDIA POST I STUMBLED UPON WHILE ENJOYING MY MORNING COFFEE BEFORE SETTING OFF ON THE SCHOOL RUN!"

Kate Russell

existing brewery operations. The invaluable guidance and expertise provided by the Samuel Adams brewers, marketing team, and even the in-house electrician helped to ensure a seamless transition to a larger brewhouse and expanded production capacity.

Reflecting on her journey, Kate encourages fellow entrepreneurs to seize every opportunity that comes their way. From seeking expert advice and applying for grants to attending networking events, she underscores the importance of remaining open to possibilities.

Calling all lovers of dark beers and baking: this recipe for beer brownies is your dream come true. Years of tinkering with various beers and coffees produced this favorite version from **Kate Russell**, founder and co-owner of **Hopkinsville Brewing Company.** The dark chocolate roast of her brewery's Bell Witch Baltic Porter complements the cocoa perfectly. Serve the brownies with scoops of vanilla ice cream and pour a glass of Bell Witch Baltic Porter or your favorite dark beer.

BALTIC PORTER **BROWNIES**

1¼ cups all-purpose flour

½ cup Dutch-process cocoa powder

2 teaspoons instant espresso powder

1 teaspoon baking powder

½ teaspoon fine sea salt

1½ cups unsalted butter

2 cups semisweet chocolate chips (one 12-ounce package), divided

½ cup Hopkinsville Brewing Company Bell Witch Baltic Porter, Samuel Adams Double Bock, or other porter, or cold coffee

4 large eggs, at room temperature

½ cup granulated sugar

1 cup firmly packed light brown sugar

2 teaspoons pure vanilla extract

Preheat the oven to 350°F. Spray the bottom and sides of a 9 x 13-inch baking pan lightly with cooking spray. Line the bottom and sides of the pan with parchment paper, and lightly spray the parchment paper with cooking spray.

To mix the dry ingredients, in a medium bowl, sift together the flour, cocoa powder, espresso powder, baking powder, and salt.

To make the chocolate-beer mixture, in a saucepan over medium-low heat, melt the butter. Add ½ cup of the chocolate chips and heat, stirring, just until melted. Remove from the heat and stir in the beer, mixing well.

To assemble the batter, in a large bowl, using an electric mixer or a whisk, beat together the eggs, both sugars, and the vanilla until the sugars dissolve and the mixture is well blended and thick, about 2 minutes. Add the chocolate-beer mixture and beat to combine. Add the flour mixture and beat on low speed or stir until well mixed. Stir in ½ cup of the chocolate chips.

To bake the brownies, pour the batter into the prepared pan and spread evenly. Sprinkle the remaining 1 cup chocolate chips evenly on top. Bake until the edges are firm and the center is just set, 25 to 30 minutes. Let cool completely in the pan on a wire rack before cutting to serve. To store leftover brownies, cover the pan with plastic wrap and keep at room temperature for up to 1 week.

Makes 8 servings

Making cheesecake from scratch can be time-consuming. This easy-to-make, no-bake cheesecake dip from **Jenifer Shwartz,** founder of **Freezcake,** gives you all of the flavor and creamy luxury of a cheesecake without all the work. It's perfect for parties, get-togethers, or when you feel like a delicious treat. Add your own personal touch with a selection of fresh, seasonal fruit, sweet crackers, and plain cookies.

CHEESECAKE DIP

1 (8-ounce) package cream cheese, cut into pieces, at room temperature

¼ cup whole milk

1 cup powdered sugar

2 teaspoons pure vanilla extract

1 (1.6-ounce) bag New York Freezcake

Dipper Suggestions

Fresh fruit, small whole or halved strawberries, raspberries, or apple or pear slices

Graham crackers

Pretzels

Vanilla sugar cookies or wafers

Cinnamon-sugar pita chips

To make the dip, in a bowl, using an electric mixer, beat together the cream cheese and milk on medium-high speed until smooth and creamy. Sift the powdered sugar over the mixture. On medium speed, beat until the sugar is fully incorporated and the mixture is smooth, then beat in the vanilla.

To add the Freezcake, with the mixer on low speed, beat in the Freezcake just until evenly distributed. You can leave the Freezcake lightly crushed or continue to beat until the dip is completely smooth. (This dip can also be made in a food processor, adding the ingredients in the same order and processing after each addition as directed.)

To serve, scoop the dip into a serving bowl and serve with the desired dippers.

Sherronda Daye formed the idea for her company, **Defense Tea**, during the COVID-19 pandemic. Using her expertise in chemistry and health, she developed a line of teas and other products that promote well-being by strengthening the immune system. This delicious recipe is easy to make, and according to Sherronda, these peanut buttery, chocolate chip–packed oat cookies will "start a party in your mouth."

OATMEAL, PEANUT BUTTER & CHOCOLATE CHIP **COOKIES**

Position two oven racks in the center of the oven and preheat the oven to 350°F. Line two sheet pans with parchment paper.

To mix the dry ingredients, in a medium bowl, whisk together the flour, baking powder, baking soda, and salt.

To cream the butter and sugar, in a large bowl, using an electric mixer, beat the butter on medium-high speed until smooth, about 1 minute. Add both sugars and continue to beat on medium-high speed until light and fluffy, about 3 minutes.

Add the eggs one at a time, beating after each addition until incorporated. Add the peanut butter and vanilla and beat until blended. Stop the mixer and scrape down the sides and along the bottom of the bowl.

To finish the cookie dough, on low speed, add the flour mixture and beat just until incorporated. Turn off the mixer. Using a rubber spatula, gently stir in the oats and then fold in the chocolate chips until evenly distributed. The dough will be thick and sticky.

Cover the bowl and refrigerate for at least 25 minutes or up to overnight.

To scoop the cookies, using a medium cookie scoop, scoop up balls of dough and arrange them on the prepared sheet pan, spacing them about 2 inches apart.

Bake the cookies, switching the pans between the racks and rotating them back to front at the halfway point, until lightly browned on the edges, 8 to 11 minutes. The centers will look very soft. Let cool in the pan on a wire rack for 5 minutes, then transfer the cookies to the rack and let cool completely. The cookies will keep in an airtight container at room temperature for up to 4 days.

1½ cups all-purpose flour

1 teaspoon baking powder

1 teaspoon baking soda

1 teaspoon fine sea salt

1 cup unsalted butter, at room temperature

¾ cup granulated sugar

¾ cup firmly packed light or dark brown sugar

2 large eggs, at room temperature

1½ cups creamy peanut butter

2 teaspoons pure vanilla extract

2 cups old-fashioned rolled oats

2½ cups semisweet chocolate chips

This updated version of apple pie comes from multitalented artist, cake designer, and baker **Ché Houston,** founder of **Ché René Macarons & More** in Atlanta. Here, she makes use of graham cracker crumbs in the crust, the filling, and the crunchy topping in this vegan-friendly riff on a classic apple dessert. Ché prefers tart-sweet Granny Smith apples for the filling, but you can instead use Braeburn, Honeycrisp, or Pink Lady.

VEGAN **APPLE CRUMBLE PIE**

Preheat the oven to 350°F.

To make the crust, in a bowl, stir together the graham cracker crumbs, sugar, and butter until the mixture is evenly moistened. Transfer the crumb mixture to a 9-inch pie pan. Using the bottom of a dry measuring cup, press the mixture firmly and evenly onto the bottom and up the sides of the pan.

To make the filling, in a large saucepan over medium-high heat, melt the butter. Add the apples, sugar, flour, and apple pie spice and stir to combine. Cook, stirring occasionally, until the sugar has dissolved, the apples are tender, and the mixture has thickened and looks like a chunky applesauce, 7 to 10 minutes. Remove from the heat.

To make the crumble topping, in a bowl, stir together the butter, graham cracker crumbs, sugar, and cinnamon.

Scoop the warm filling into the pie crust and top evenly with the crumble mixture.

Bake the pie until the top browns and crisps, about 7 minutes. Let cool on a wire rack until warm, then cut and serve, topping each wedge with a big scoop of ice cream.

Pie Crust

2 cups vegan graham cracker crumbs

2 tablespoons sugar

4 tablespoons vegan butter, melted

Apple Filling

4 tablespoons vegan butter

5 Granny Smith apples, peeled, cored, and cut into ½-inch chunks

1 cup sugar

⅓ cup all-purpose flour

1 tablespoon apple pie spice

Crumble Topping

4 tablespoons vegan butter, melted

1 cup vegan graham cracker crumbs

1 tablespoon sugar

1 teaspoon ground cinnamon

Vegan vanilla ice cream or whipped cream, for serving

A delightful blend of velvety sweet potatoes and aromatic spices come together in this favorite recipe of **Deborah Smalls,** founder of **Sweet Carolina Pies,** based in New York City. Be sure to use orange-fleshed sweet potatoes, which are sweeter and more tender than the white or purple varieties. If you are too pressed for time to make a pie crust, try to find an all-butter one at the store.

SWEET POTATO PIE

1 pound medium-size orange-fleshed sweet potatoes

1 cup sugar

2 large eggs, lightly beaten

½ cup unsalted butter, melted

1 teaspoon pure vanilla extract

½ cup evaporated milk

1 tablespoon all-purpose flour

½ teaspoon ground cinnamon

¼ teaspoon ground nutmeg

¼ teaspoon ground ginger

¼ teaspoon fine sea salt

9-inch unbaked pie crust, homemade or store-bought

Whipped cream, for serving (optional)

Preheat the oven to 325°F. Line a sheet pan with aluminum foil.

To bake the sweet potatoes, prick them all over with the tines of a fork. Set them on the prepared sheet pan and bake until very tender and a fork easily slides into a potato with no resistance, about 45 minutes. Remove from the oven and let cool until they can be handled.

Peel the sweet potatoes, discard the skins, and drop the flesh into a large bowl.

Mash the sweet potatoes until smooth; you should have about 2 cups. Add the sugar, eggs, melted butter, and vanilla and stir to combine. Add the evaporated milk, flour, cinnamon, nutmeg, ginger, and salt and stir until well mixed and smooth.

Reduce the oven temperature to 300°F. Line the sheet pan with fresh aluminum foil. Pour the pie filling into the pie crust.

Bake the pie until a toothpick inserted into the center comes out mostly clean, 55 to 60 minutes. Let cool on a wire rack to room temperature. Serve at room temperature or refrigerate and serve chilled. Top each serving with whipped cream, if desired.

SAMUEL ADAMS
WINTER LAGER

Our end-of-the-year star is Winter Lager, brewed with cinnamon and orange peel to brighten your holiday season. With festive flavors and the smoothness of a sleigh ride, our full-bodied lager will be comfortable company on the cold days of November and December. Just a touch of bitterness will balance out the melody, chased away by the warm finish of citrus and cinnamon. Spice up your traditions with a Winter Lager as you ring in the New Year and await warmer days.

MAKES 1 ALE-TAIL
WINTER LAGER EGGNOG

2½ ounces Samuel Adams Winter Lager
1 ounce dark rum
1 ounce apple brandy
1 barspoon honey
1 large egg
Ground cinnamon, for garnish

Chill a martini glass or champagne coupe. In a cocktail shaker, combine the lager, rum, apple brandy, and honey and stir with a barspoon until the carbonation subsides. Add the egg to the shaker, fill the shaker half full of ice, cover, and shake vigorously until the outside of the shaker is frosty, 10 to 15 seconds. Strain the cocktail into a tumbler, discard the ice, then return the liquid to the shaker, re-cover, and shake vigorously with no ice for 1 minute, or until frothy. Pour into the chilled glass, garnish with cinnamon, and serve.

This rustic and less-than-sweet cheesecake from **Kurt Beecher Dammeier,** founder of **Beecher's Handmade Cheese,** uses Beecher's honey-oat crackers for the crust and Beecher's Flagship cheese, a semihard cow's milk cheese, with creamy mascarpone and lemon for the filling. A splash of Samuel Adams Summer Ale gives the raspberry layer an extraordinary flavor and brings a balancing bitterness to the sweet berry sauce.

MASCARPONE **RASPBERRY CHEESECAKE**

To make the crust, preheat the oven to 350°F. In a food processor, combine the crackers and brown sugar and process until fine, even crumbs form, about 30 seconds. Add the melted butter in a steady stream while pulsing, until the mixture is evenly moistened and sticks together when pressed between your fingers. Transfer the crumb mixture to a 9-inch pie pan. Using the bottom of a dry measuring cup, press the mixture firmly and evenly onto the bottom and up the sides of the pan. Use the back of a spoon to create an even edge.

Bake the crust until fragrant and golden brown, 12 to 18 minutes. Let cool on a wire rack to room temperature, about 30 minutes.

Make the mascarpone filling while the crust is cooling. In a small, microwave-safe bowl, sprinkle the gelatin evenly over the lemon juice and set aside to bloom for 10 minutes. Place the gelatin mixture in the microwave and heat on high power until steaming, about 30 seconds. Let cool to room temperature.

In a large bowl, using a rubber spatula, stir together the mascarpone and ½ cup of the powdered sugar, mixing well. In a medium bowl, whisk together the cream and the remaining 2 tablespoons powdered sugar until soft peaks form. Stir the cooled gelatin mixture into the mascarpone mixture, then stir in the grated cheese. Gently fold in the whipped cream just until incorporated.

Transfer the mascarpone filling to the cooled crust. Using a spoon, spread the filling to the edges to create a 1-inch lip with an indentation in the center. Cover and refrigerate until set, about 2 hours.

To make the raspberry filling, in a small bowl, sprinkle the gelatin evenly over the lemon juice and set aside for 10 minutes. In a saucepan over medium-high heat, simmer the beer for 3 minutes. Add the brown sugar and salt and, using a heat-resistant spatula, stir to dissolve. Add the raspberries and stir, mashing them slightly with the spatula. Cook the mixture, stirring occasionally, until thickened and the spatula leaves a trail when drawn across the bottom of the pan, about 10 minutes. Stir in the gelatin mixture, immediately remove from the heat, and transfer to a heatproof bowl. Let cool to room temperature.

Pour the cooled raspberry filling into the indentation in the mascarpone filling. Cover and refrigerate until the raspberry filling has lightly set, at least 1 hour or until ready to serve. Just before serving, garnish with the raspberries, arranging them around the edge of the cheesecake.

Crust

1 (5-ounce) package Beecher's Honey Oat Crackers or Wheat Thins

¼ cup light brown sugar

5 tablespoons unsalted butter, melted and cooled

Mascarpone Filling

1 teaspoon powdered gelatin

¼ cup fresh lemon juice

1½ cups (12 ounces) mascarpone cheese

½ cup plus 2 tablespoons powdered sugar

1 cup heavy cream

6 ounces Beecher's Flagship cheese or aged white Cheddar, coarsely grated

Raspberry Filling

½ teaspoon powdered gelatin

1 teaspoon fresh lemon juice

¾ cup Samuel Adams Summer Ale or other citrus wheat beer

5 tablespoons firmly packed light brown sugar

Pinch of kosher salt

12 ounces fresh raspberries, plus 6 ounces for garnish

★ BREWER'S FAVORITE ★

This simple yet impressive cake is perfect for the holidays or festive get-togethers. The addition of Samuel Adams Black Lager or Cinnamon Roll Breakfast Bock paired with dark and sticky molasses adds extra depth and moisture to this spicy treat. You can use any shape 12-cup Bundt-style pan you'd like, just be sure to grease and flour it well before baking. For an extra special dessert, serve this drizzled with salted caramel sauce and scoops of Vanilla Porter Ice Cream (page 215).

GINGERBREAD BUNDT CAKE

1 cup unsalted butter, at room temperature, plus more for the pan

2½ cups all-purpose flour, plus more for the pan

2 teaspoons baking soda

2 teaspoons ground ginger

2 teaspoons ground cinnamon

½ teaspoon ground cloves

½ teaspoon fine sea salt

1¼ cups firmly packed light brown sugar

3 large eggs, at room temperature

1 cup dark molasses (not blackstrap)

¾ cup Samuel Adams Black Lager or Cinnamon Roll Breakfast Bock, flat, at room temperature

Powdered sugar, for dusting

Preheat the oven to 350°F. Generously grease a 12-cup Bundt or other fluted cake pan with butter, then dust with flour, tapping out the excess.

To make the cake batter, in a medium bowl, sift together the flour, baking soda, ginger, cinnamon, cloves, and salt. In a large bowl, using an electric mixer, beat together the butter and brown sugar on high speed until fluffy, about 1 minute. Beat in the eggs one at a time, beating after each addition until incorporated. Add the molasses and beat until blended. (The batter may look curdled at this stage, but it will be fine.) On low speed, beat in one-third of the flour mixture until incorporated, then stop the mixer and scrape down the sides of the bowl. Repeat with the remaining flour mixture in two batches, stopping to scrape down the sides of the bowl as needed. Add the lager and beat until incorporated.

Scrape the batter into the prepared pan and smooth the top.

Bake the cake until a toothpick inserted near the center comes out clean, 50 to 60 minutes. Let cool in the pan on a wire rack for 10 minutes, then unmold the cake onto the rack. Enjoy warm or let cool completely. Dust with powdered sugar before serving.

This mixed-juice drink from **Dominique Burrell-Paige,** founder of California-based **Blacker the Berry Juicery,** will have your taste buds singing. In addition to producing a colorful selection of delicious, cold-pressed, 100 percent plant-based juices, her company is dedicated to ensuring people living in marginalized communities have greater access to healthy food choices. You'll need a juicer and some fresh, ripe fruit to create this vitamin-packed drink.

GRAPE ESCAPE

2 ripe Anjou pears,
cut into chunks

1 Cara Cara orange,
cut into chunks

½ pink grapefruit,
cut into chunks

¼-inch piece fresh ginger

To prepare the drink, feed the pears, orange, grapefruit, and ginger into the feeding tube of your juicer, alternating hard and soft pieces of fruit to get the most juice out. If using a conventional juicer, the juice is best drunk within 24 hours. If using a cold-press juicer, it can be refrigerated in an airtight container for up to 1 week.

Known for its rich flavor and thick consistency, this Venezuelan-style hot chocolate feels like a warm hug with every sip. Although Venezuela sits on the Caribbean side of South America, much of its territory is in the Andean region of high, snow-covered peaks, which is where this hot chocolate originates. Venezuelan-born **Aura Fajardo,** founder of **Aura's Chocolate Bar** in Rhode Island, likes to make it with a special twist: a generous amount of cinnamon, a little sea salt, and a pinch of cayenne pepper for a touch of spiciness. It is wonderful served with churros for dipping. Aura doesn't add sugar, but the kids often like it a little sweeter.

VENEZUELAN **HOT CHOCOLATE**

To melt the chocolate, put it into a microwave-safe bowl and microwave on high in 20-second bursts, stirring after each burst, until melted and smooth. (Alternatively, melt the chocolate in a small saucepan over low heat, stirring occasionally, until smooth.)

To make the hot chocolate, in a saucepan over low heat, whisk together the milk, cornstarch, and sugar (if using) until the mixture is smooth. Stir in the melted chocolate, cinnamon, and salt and continue cooking, stirring constantly, until the mixture thickens to the consistency of heavy cream, about 5 minutes. Taste and add more sugar if needed.

Ladle the hot chocolate into mugs and sprinkle each serving with cinnamon and—if feeling adventurous—a tiny pinch of cayenne.

10 ounces bittersweet chocolate, preferably Aura's Dark 73.5 percent, chopped

4 cups whole milk, or more depending on desired consistency

2 tablespoons cornstarch

1 tablespoon sugar, or more to taste (optional)

1 teaspoon ground cinnamon, plus more for sprinkling

Pinch of fine sea salt

Cayenne pepper, for sprinkling (optional)

This refreshing vegan drink from **Andre Marrero** of **Nantucket Faraway Chocolate** is reminiscent of an old-fashioned chocolate soda but updated to today's tastes. You can use a good-quality bittersweet chocolate bar, preferably from his upscale chocolate company, instead of chocolate syrup. Just melt ¼ cup of the chopped chocolate in a saucepan with the almond milk, then chill the mixture before proceeding.

CHOCOLATE ALMOND **COOLER**

½ cup almond milk

¼ cup good-quality bittersweet chocolate syrup

1 teaspoon instant espresso powder

Pinch of fine sea salt

1 cup club soda

Fill a cocktail shaker half full of ice. Add the almond milk, chocolate syrup, espresso powder, and salt, cover, and shake vigorously until the outside of the shaker is frosty, 10 to 15 seconds.

Fill two tall glasses with ice. Strain the almond milk mixture into the glasses, dividing it evenly. Top off with the club soda, dividing it evenly, and serve.

★ BREWER'S FAVORITE ★

Ice cream infused with Samuel Adams Oaked Vanilla Porter boasts a rich, malty flavor with hints of vanilla. Enjoy it solo for a decadent dessert or pair with warm Baltic Porter Brownies (page 200) for a delightful sundae. For a boozy twist, drizzle with caramel whiskey sauce or top with candied nuts for added texture and crunch.

VANILLA PORTER **ICE CREAM**

To make the ice cream, in a saucepan over low heat, simmer the porter until reduced to 2 cups. Meanwhile, fill a large bowl with ice cubes and water. When the porter is reduced, add the heavy cream and half of the sugar and stir to mix. Using the back of a paring knife, scrape the seeds from the vanilla bean pod and add the seeds and pod to the cream mixture. Increase the heat to medium and bring the mixture to a gentle boil, stirring until smooth. Remove from the heat.

In a heatproof bowl, whisk together the whole eggs, egg yolks, the remaining sugar, and the salt. While whisking constantly, slowly pour the hot cream mixture into the egg mixture, continuing to whisk until well blended. Strain the mixture though a fine-mesh sieve into a medium bowl and rest the bowl in the ice bath. Let the ice cream base cool, stirring occasionally, until well chilled.

Pour the chilled ice cream base into an ice cream maker and freeze according to the manufacturer's instructions. Transfer to an airtight container and place in the freezer until firm, at least 2 hours. It will keep for up to 2 weeks.

4 cups Samuel Adams Oaked Vanilla Porter, Black Lager, or Cinnamon Roll Breakfast Bock

2 cups heavy cream

1 cup sugar

1 vanilla bean, split lengthwise

3 large whole eggs

7 large egg yolks

1 teaspoon fine sea salt

In this recipe, **Uli Nasibova,** founder of **Uli's Gelato** in Los Angeles, infuses creamy, rich, dense gelato with fragrant honey. Because she calls for only a handful of ingredients, be sure to source the best you can find. Keep in mind, too, that the variety of honey you use, such as clover, orange blossom, wildflower, or dandelion, will dictate the overall flavor of this frozen treat. Uli includes the seeds of a vanilla bean for another layer of flavor, which can be traded out for 1 teaspoon vanilla paste. She tops the gelato with crunchy toasted pistachios, but you can leave the gelato as is for pure bliss.

HONEY GELATO WITH PISTACHIOS

To infuse the milk, in a heavy saucepan over low heat, combine the honey and water, stirring until warm and well blended. Using the back of a paring knife, scrape the seeds from the vanilla bean pod and add the seeds and pod to the honey mixture along with the salt. Pour in the milk, increase the heat to medium, and bring the mixture to a simmer, stirring until smooth and the mixture registers 170°F on an instant-read thermometer. Remove from the heat, cover, and set aside for 1 hour.

Fill a large bowl with ice cubes and water.

To finish the gelato base, in a heatproof bowl, whisk the eggs yolks until blended. While whisking constantly, pour the cooled milk mixture into the yolks. Return the mixture to the saucepan, place over low heat, and warm, stirring constantly, until it registers 185°F on the instant-read thermometer. Remove from the heat, strain through a fine-mesh sieve into a medium bowl, and rest the bowl in the ice bath. Let cool completely, stirring occasionally.

When the mixture is cool, remove the bowl from the ice bath and stir in the heavy cream. Cover the bowl and chill the mixture overnight in the refrigerator.

Pour the chilled base into a gelato or ice cream maker and freeze according to the manufacturer's instructions. Transfer the gelato to an airtight container, press plastic wrap onto the surface of the gelato, then cover with the lid.

Scoop the gelato into individual bowls, sprinkle with the pistachios, and serve.

½ cup honey

¼ cup water

1 vanilla bean, split lengthwise

¼ teaspoon fine sea salt

2 cups whole milk

4 large egg yolks

1 cup heavy cream

1 cup shelled pistachios, for garnish

Sheet cakes are an ideal dessert to take to a potluck or picnic since they travel well in the baking pan. This recipe from **Lonnie Dutton** of the **Texas Cannon Brewing Company** based in Blanco, Texas, gets its rich, malty flavors from a healthy dose of Samuel Adams Chocolate Bock beer in both the cake and the frosting. Serve the cake on its own or with a scoop of your favorite ice cream.

CHOCOLATE BOCK **SHEET CAKE**

Sheet Cake

1 cup unsalted butter, plus room-temperature butter for the baking pan

2 cups all-purpose flour, plus more for the baking pan

1 cup Samuel Adams Chocolate Bock or Double Bock

3 tablespoons unsweetened natural cocoa powder

2 cups granulated sugar

1 teaspoon baking soda

1 teaspoon fine sea salt

½ cup buttermilk

2 large eggs

1 teaspoon pure vanilla extract

Frosting

½ cup unsalted butter

6 tablespoons Samuel Adams Chocolate Bock or Double Bock

3 tablespoons unsweetened natural cocoa powder

1 teaspoon pure vanilla extract

2 cups powdered sugar

Your favorite flavor ice cream, for serving (optional)

To prepare the cake pan, preheat the oven to 350°F. Grease the bottom and sides of a 9 x 13-inch baking pan or dish with butter, then dust with flour, tapping out the excess.

To make the cocoa-beer mixture, in a saucepan over medium heat, melt the 1 cup butter. Add the beer and cocoa powder and whisk to mix well. Cook, stirring constantly, until the mixture comes to a boil. Remove from the heat and let cool slightly.

To finish the cake batter, in a large bowl, whisk together the 2 cups flour, granulated sugar, baking soda, and salt. In a medium bowl, whisk together the buttermilk, eggs, and vanilla until blended. Add the beer mixture to the buttermilk mixture and whisk to combine. Add the wet ingredients to the flour mixture and stir just until thoroughly blended.

To bake the cake, pour the batter into the prepared pan. Bake the cake until a toothpick inserted into the center comes out clean, about 30 minutes. Let cool in the pan on a wire rack while you make the frosting.

To make the frosting, in a saucepan over medium heat, melt the butter. Remove the pan from the heat and add the beer, cocoa powder, and vanilla. Whisk until blended. Add the powdered sugar and whisk until smooth.

Spread the frosting over the warm cake. Let the cake cool completely before serving. Serve with scoops of ice cream, if you like.

CARLENE O'GARRO, FOUNDER OF DELECTABLE DESIRES PASTRIES

Born and raised in Boston, Carlene grew up in a Caribbean household. Her mother is from Barbados, and her father is from Montserrat. Both her parents worked, but her mother always made sure there was a hot meal for breakfast, lunch, and dinner. Like many first-generation immigrant children, Carlene had parents who instilled in her the value of a good education and the importance of a stable career. She graduated from college with a bachelor's degree, but after taking the LSAT and applying to law school, she decided to follow her passion and become a pastry chef. The idea was daunting, but she enrolled in the Cambridge School of Culinary Arts and trained as a French pastry chef. Her decision to switch from lawyer to pastry chef was to ensure a career that would bring her peace, joy, and happiness. The happiness she felt as a child on Sundays in the kitchen with her mother is the same happiness she's been blessed with since taking the leap and launching Delectable Desires Pastries in 2007.

Carlene knew she had a talent for baking and creating delicious desserts, but she didn't have the acumen to run a business. She started her bakery business only three months after graduating from culinary school, and while her business grew in the next year, she was having trouble paying her vendors because her clients weren't paying her on time.

Right around this time Carlene met Jim Koch and the team at Brewing the American Dream. They happened to be neighbors in the same building complex in Jamaica Plain. Within a couple of weeks, she became their first entrepreneur and received her first loan for $2,500. The loan came with an education on how to run a business. The Brewing the American Dream team advised on how to set terms, ways of collecting payment, when to

"MY ADVICE TO OTHER ENTREPRENEURS IS TO KEEP PUSHING YOURSELF AND NEVER STOP LEARNING AND GROWING. IT'S YOUR DREAM, AND IF YOU BELIEVE IN IT, THERE IS NO LIMIT. "

Carlene O'Garro

stop supplying clients with products until payment was received, drawing up contracts, branding, and marketing. From her first loan in 2008 to her last loan in 2018, her perception of talent and business changed for the better.

In 2014, Carlene took a leap and opened her first storefront location in West Roxbury, Massachusetts. Her little shop has had big results, from cranking out more than five thousand pies in the fall months to producing showstopping cakes. She feels lucky to share so many moments with customers who've turned into friends or have become like family, and continues to have a close relationship with the Brewing the American Dream organization through mentorship, networking, and partnership.

During her early days of baking at home, perfecting buttercream seemed an arduous task to **Carlene O'Garro**. But more than seventeen years of experience (and plenty of trial and error) produced this light and fluffy recipe that strikes the ideal balance of sweet, salt, and buttery. Here, her Swiss meringue buttercream is used to fill and coat a towering lemon-scented layer cake that includes both raspberry jam and fresh raspberries between the layers—perfect for any celebration. This versatile buttercream can be used for virtually any frosting job, including macarons and whoopie pies. Try Carlene's favorite, in which her luscious buttercream is sandwiched between two jumbo chocolate chip cookies.

LEMON RASPBERRY CELEBRATION CAKE
WITH VANILLA BUTTERCREAM

Lemon Cake

¾ cup unsalted butter, cut into chunks, at room temperature, plus more for the pans

3 cups cake flour, plus more for the pans

2 teaspoons baking powder

1 teaspoon baking soda

1 teaspoon fine sea salt

1¾ cups granulated sugar

⅓ cup canola oil

1 packed tablespoon finely grated lemon zest (from 2 large lemons)

4 large eggs

2 egg yolks

1 teaspoon lemon extract

1 cup sour cream

Lemon Cake Syrup

½ cup granulated sugar

½ cup fresh lemon juice

To prep the cake pans, preheat the oven to 350°F. Lightly grease the bottom and sides of two 9-inch round cake pans with butter. Line the bottoms with parchment paper, grease the parchment with butter, and then dust the bottoms and sides with flour and tap out the excess.

To make the cake batter, whisk together the 3 cups flour, baking powder, baking soda, and salt. In a stand mixer fitted with the beater attachment, beat together the granulated sugar, ¾ cup butter, oil, and lemon zest on low speed until blended. Increase the speed to high and beat until light and fluffy, about 2 minutes. Add the eggs and egg yolks one at a time, beating after each addition, until incorporated. Stop the mixer and scrape down the sides of the bowl with a rubber spatula. On low speed, beat in the lemon extract, then add the sour cream and beat until well mixed. On low speed, slowly add the flour mixture and mix just until incorporated. Turn off the mixer. Using the rubber spatula, give the batter one last stir to make sure the batter is well mixed. Do not overmix.

To bake the cake layers, divide the batter evenly between the prepared pans and spread into an even layer. Bake until golden and a toothpick inserted into the center of a cake layer comes out clean, 35 to 40 minutes. Let cool in the pans on wire racks for 20 minutes, then invert the cakes onto the racks, lift off the pans, and peel off the parchment. Let cool completely.

To make the cake syrup, combine the sugar and lemon juice in a small saucepan and place over medium heat. Bring to a boil, whisking until the sugar dissolves. Remove from the heat and let cool completely.

continued...

...continued

Vanilla Buttercream

4 ounces (½ cup) pasteurized egg whites, at room temperature

1 pound (4 cups) powdered sugar

2 teaspoons pure vanilla extract

½ teaspoon fine sea salt

2 cups (1 pound) unsalted butter, cut into pieces, at cool room temperature

Filling and Decorating

9 tablespoons raspberry jam

12 ounces fresh raspberries, halved

Edible or food-grade flowers

To make the buttercream, wash and dry the mixer bowl and beater attachment, then return the bowl to the mixer stand and fit the mixer with the beater attachment. Add the egg whites to the bowl and sift the powdered sugar over the egg whites. Beat on low speed until blended. Increase the speed to high and beat until the sugar is fully dissolved, 1 to 2 minutes. You do not need to whip to a meringue. Add the vanilla and salt and beat to combine. With the mixture on, slowly add the butter. When all the butter is added, continue to beat on high speed until the buttercream is white and fluffy, 8 to 10 minutes.

To assemble the cake, cut each cake in half horizontally to make two even layers; you should have a total of four 9-inch round layers. Place one 9-inch cake layer, bottom side down, on a 10-inch cardboard cake round. Brush the cake layer generously with the lemon cake syrup. Spread a thin layer of the raspberry jam (about 3 tablespoons) on the cake layer, then spread about ½ cup of the frosting over the top. Add about one-third of the raspberries on top, spacing them evenly.

Place a second cake layer on top. As before, brush the second cake layer with the syrup, spread with jam, frost with the buttercream, and top with fresh rapberries. Repeat for the third cake layer. Place the fourth cake layer on top, bottom side up, and brush the top of the cake with simple syrup.

For the crumb coat, spread a thin layer of buttercream all over the sides and top of the cake. Refrigerate the cake for about 20 minutes.

To finish and decorate the cake, remove it from the refrigerator and frost with a second, thicker layer of buttercream. Decorate the top with flowers. Cut into wedges to serve. The cake can be assembled but not decorated up to 1 day in advance and refrigerated. Bring to room temperature and decorate before serving.

Steeping **El Colombiano Coffee** cold brew—or your favorite blend—draws out the coffee's full flavor and makes it smoother, milder, and less acidic than the traditional hot-brewed beverage. To serve it on its own, add milk or sweeten if desired and serve it over ice. El Colombiano founder **Javier Amador-Peña** likes transforming cold brew into an upscale cocktail with his freshly made cold brew, adding a twist to a classic negroni. The bitterness of the coffee complements the herbal and citrus notes in the drink. Cheers!

COLD BREW NEGRONI
WITH COLD BREW COFFEE

To make the cold brew, combine the coffee and water in a glass jar. Cover and let steep for 18 hours at room temperature. Line a drip coffee filter with a paper filter and set over a glass jar or other container. Pour the cold brew concentrate through the filter. Adjust the amount of water to your desired strength. The cold brew will keep in a tightly capped jar or other container in the refrigerator for up to 2 days.

To make the cocktail, fill a rocks glass with ice cubes. Pour the gin, Campari, vermouth, and cold brew over the ice and give everything a quick stir. Add a twist of orange zest for garnish and serve.

Cold Brew Coffee

1 ounce coarsely ground El Colombiano Coffee Cold Brew blend or your favorite ground coffee

½ cup filtered water, at room temperature

Cocktail

1 ounce gin or bourbon

1 ounce Campari

1 ounce sweet vermouth

1 ounce cold brew coffee, preferably El Colombiano Coffee

Orange zest strip, for garnish

HOW TO APPRAISE BEER

STEP 1:
APPEARANCE
TAKE A LOOK AT THE BEER

Note the head on the beer:
• Does it remain or does it dissipate quickly?
• How thick is it?

What color is the beer?
• Golden, amber, brown?

What is the clarity of the beer?
• Can you see through it?
• Is it cloudy?

STEP 2:
AROMA
SMELL THE BEER FOR BOUQUET

Do you detect aromas such as caramel, chocolate, or toffee?

Do you detect hop aromas that are flowery, herbal, fruity, or grassy?

Do you detect yeast aromas such as banana or clove?

Are there any off-flavors?
• Flavors like spoiled veggies, movie buttered popcorn, wet cardboard, or vinegar could indicate an issue

STEP 3:
TASTE
THE MOMENT OF TRUTH

What tastes are on your palate?
• Sweetness from the malt?
• Bitterness from the hops?

Is the taste balanced or is there more of an accent on the malt or hops?

Does it taste fresh?

STEP 4:
MOUTHFEEL
REFERS TO THE BODY OF THE BEER

Is it thin and watery or does it fill your mouth with flavor?

What is the texture of the beer?
• Creamy, effervescent, etc.

In some cases, flat beer or a "slick" coating can indicate a quality issue.

STEP 5:
FINISH
DO YOU WANT MORE?

Does the taste linger on your palate or disappear quickly?

Most importantly, does it make you want to take another sip?

BREWING THE AMERICAN DREAM
TRAILBLAZERS

INDEX

salsas

    Charred Salsa Verde with
Chunky Avocado, 32

    Roasted Tomato Salsa, 33

Sambuxas with Feta & Dill, 42

Samuel Adams Black Lager

    Beer-Braised Pork with
BBQ Sauce, 140

    Black Lager Floats with
Mascarpone Ice Cream, 195

    Braised Red Cabbage with
Beer & Apples, 165

    Gingerbread Bundt Cake, 210

    Ginger Steamed Fish
with Porter, 147

    Pork Tenderloin with
Citrus-Beer Brine, 149

    Vanilla Porter Ice Cream, 215

Samuel Adams Boston Lager, 15, 16

    Bacon Burgers with
Boston Lager, 95

    BBQ Pizza with Braised Pork, 50

    Beer Can Chicken, 110

    Beer Cheese with Boston Lager, 35

    Beer-Poached Shrimp Cocktail, 56

    Boston Lager Baked Beans, 158

    Boston Lager Chili Sauce, 94

    Brat Sandwiches with
Peppers & Onions, 98

    Brussels Sprouts with
Bacon & OctoberFest, 170

    Chicken Kebabs with
Beer-Bourbon Marinade, 121

    Chicken Wings with Smoky Beer
Marinade, 46

    Crab Fritters with Boston Lager, 57

    Farmhouse Reuben, 86

    Fish & Chips, 105

    Grilled Lobster with Tomato
Vinaigrette, 135

    Grilled Shrimp with
Beer & Lemon Marinade, 143

    Jambalaya with Sausage &
Boston Lager, 141

Kale Salad with OctoberFest
Vinaigrette, 83

    Pasta with Eggplant,
Ham & Lager, 146

    Risotto with Beer & Parmesan, 176

    Warm Potato Salad with Beer
Dressing, 164

Samuel Adams Chocolate Bock

    Beer-Braised Pork with
BBQ Sauce, 140

    Bock-Glazed Carrots with
Yogurt, Harissa & Herbs, 172

    Chocolate Bock Sheet Cake, 218

    Pork Chops with Mustard &
Onions, 116

Samuel Adams Cinnamon Roll
Breakfast Bock

    Beer-Braised Pork with
BBQ Sauce, 140

    Black Lager Floats with
Mascarpone Ice Cream, 195

    Bock-Glazed Carrots with Yogurt,
Harissa & Herbs, 172

    Gingerbread Bundt Cake, 210

    Vanilla Porter Ice Cream, 215

Samuel Adams Cold Snap, 77

    Cold Snap Bee's Knees, 77

Samuel Adams Double Bock

    Baltic Porter Brownies, 200

    Beer-Glazed Onions, 177

    Black Lager Floats with
Mascarpone Ice Cream, 195

    Braised Red Cabbage with
Beer & Apples, 165

    Chocolate Bock Sheet Cake, 218

Samuel Adams Golden Pilsner

    Fish & Chips, 105

Samuel Adams Oaked Vanilla Porter

    Beer-Glazed Onions, 177

    Ginger Steamed Fish with
Porter, 147

    Pork Tenderloin with
Citrus-Beer Brine, 149

    Vanilla Porter Ice Cream, 215

Samuel Adams OctoberFest, 117

    Beer Can Chicken, 110

    Beer Cheese with OctoberFest, 35

    Beer-Glazed Onions, 177

    Brat Sandwiches with
Peppers & Onions, 98

    Brussels Sprouts with
Bacon & OctoberFest, 170

    Farmhouse Reuben, 86

    Grilled Lobster with Tomato
Vinaigrette, 135

    Kale Salad with OctoberFest
Vinaigrette, 83

    Meatballs with Mushroom
Beer Sauce, 122

    OctoberFest Pineapple Zinger, 117

    Pork Chops with Mustard &
Onions, 116

Samuel Adams Oyster Stout

    Braised Red Cabbage with
Beer & Apples, 165

Samuel Adams Summer Ale, 37

    Beer Can Chicken, 110

    Beer-Poached Shrimp Cocktail, 56

    Citrus Berry Refresher with
Summer Ale, 62

    Crab Fritters with Summer Ale, 57

    Focaccia with Summer Ale, 58

    Mascarpone Raspberry
Cheesecake, 209

    Risotto with Beer & Parmesan, 176

    Summer Ale Mezcal "Margarita," 37

    Summer Ale Sunset, 63

Samuel Adams Utopias, 16

Samuel Adams Wicked Easy

    Fish & Chips, 105

Samuel Adams Winter Lager, 207

    Bock-Glazed Carrots with Yogurt,
Harissa & Herbs, 172

    Pork Chops with Mustard &
Onions, 116

    Winter Lager Eggnog, 207

ACKNOWLEDGMENTS

Brewing the American Dream has been dedicated to supporting food and beverage entrepreneurs for over 15 years. With deep gratitude, we extend our thanks to Jim Koch, whose passion and vision made way for a legacy that cultivates craftsmanship in its most delicious forms.

Supporting our nation's passionate small business owners is an honor, and one we could not achieve without a truly wonderful village! First and foremost, we owe a debt of appreciation to the talented culinary trailblazers who generously shared their recipes and stories with us. Their appetite for innovation and dedication to the craft are evident in every dish. It is our hope that this book will serve as a platform for them to expand their reach and pursue their business dreams each day.

Brewing the American Dream's commitment to empowering dedicated artisans is strengthened through partnerships with nonprofit lenders like Accion Opportunity Fund, our steadfast partner since the start. Their tireless dedication to small businesses has been instrumental in the program and our entrepreneurs' success.

We also extend our thanks to the amazing partners across the country who support us year-round: 5W Public Relations, Accessity, Allies for Community Business, Ascendus, Branchfood, Build Institute, Commonwealth Kitchen, Center for Women in Enterprise, Findlay Kitchen, The Gratitude Collective, The Hatchery, Hope and Main, Hot Bread Kitchen, and Second Service Foundation.

A huge thank you to our Samuel Adams co-workers and customers for the thousands of hours of coaching, networking, and collaboration that they have given. A heartfelt thanks to Gabriel Colon-Sciabarrasi for his boundless determination, hard work, and infectious enthusiasm in supporting this program. Finally, thank you to the many Boston Beer Company colleagues who helped bring this book to life, with special recognition to Devon Savage, Brittany Zahoruiko, and the one and only Sally Jackson.

Moreover, we are deeply grateful to our publishing company, Salty Days Media Company, whose creativity, collaboration, and passion for Brewing the American Dream were indispensable in bringing this book to life. A special thank you to Publisher Sara Domville for her visionary leadership, expertise, and unwavering positivity, which have culminated in the creation of this outstanding cookbook. The invaluable guidance and relentless dedication of Editorial Director Kim Laidlaw and Creative Director Ali Zeigler were instrumental in realizing this project. We also extend our thanks to our photography and styling team, especially Photographer Michael Piazza and Food Stylists Christine Tobin, Rachel Michel, and Laura Sui, whose exceptional work breathed life into every recipe within these pages.

Thank you to our dedicated team of recipe testers: Nick, Rupert, and Benedict Domville; Elizabeth Test; William Love; and Stephen and Gregory Evans. Their valuable feedback played a crucial role in refining the recipes to ensure they meet the needs of home cooks. We also want to express our appreciation to Salty Days Media intern Humphrey Domville for his invaluable support in marketing and digital development, and to Shirley Fairclough and Marta Loeb for their creativity, expertise, and consumer survey management.

Finally, we want to express our gratitude to our readers and supporters. Your enthusiasm for cooking and support for emerging businesses will pave the way for those featured in this book and those yet to pursue their own American Dream. Thank you all for taking part in this delicious one-of-a-kind adventure!

Jennifer Glanville Love

–JENNIFER GLANVILLE LOVE

CHEERS